REDISCOVERING KINGDOM HEALING

REDISCOVERING KINGDOM HEALING

Mike Endicott

Terra Nova Publications

First Published 2006

Published in Great Britain by
Terra Nova Publications International Ltd
PO Box 2400 Bradford on Avon Wiltshire BA15 2YN

Cover image copyright © J M Byron-Davies, 2006
Cover design by Roger Judd

ISBN 1 901949 47 8

978 1 901949 47 6

Printed in Great Britain
by Bookmarque Ltd, Croydon

Contents

INTRODUCTION

The world is changing— the kingdom has come. It came with Jesus and it is still coming and will be here in its fullness when Christ returns. There are signs and wonders: signs of its being here, miracles seen in sickness; in deliverance; in raising the dead, and in natural events. All these things prevailed in the very early days of the church and for a few hundred years after Christ's ascension, but drifted gradually off the church's map, remaining for a while —mostly among the religious communities of convent and monastery. By the turn of the twentieth century they were almost unheard of amongst most church people.

As miracles through prayer became harder to come by down the intervening centuries – from Jesus' earthly ministry until the present day – proponents of the healing ministry searched for reasons for the apparent weakening of miracle working power. Much philosophising, spiritual second guessing and many secular skills have been brought to bear, to try to answer the questions and meet the situations of those who remain unhealed.

What it was believed might lead to the key has turned out to be the gaoler. The intellectual and spiritual complexity that has been built up became a thick cobweb that shielded the simplicity of kingdom miracle working from the church's eyes. Thus kingdom miracles are few and far between.

But now this open secret of kingdom living has been rediscovered. Each Christian may have a story to tell which can reach hundreds of others. Tools have been found to strip away the cobwebs that have clouded the ministry of Christian healing and had confined it to a dark corner of ineffectiveness and controversy.

Now there is a great harvest of fruit again. Now it is possible to rediscover the power of the message of the cross, together with every Christian's authority and ability to put it to work —out of our compassion for the sick and our love of Christ.

Chapter One

A GLIMPSE OF THE PROMISED LAND

For one exciting reason I came home to my garden today full of the joy of heaven. There was a definite bounce in my step, and a sense in the air that spring had at long last begun to turn her face towards our neck of the woods. And so it has been with miracles in the church's ministry to the sick and the injured! A fresh season seems to be coming to the church's healing ministry. People are receiving miracles again, in large enough numbers to be noticed at last.

It has been a long, struggling and often fruitless winter that has sometimes seemed never-ending. The early summer has arrived. In some parts of the country, as in some parts of the church's healing ministry, the temporal and spiritual weather has been actually, as well as metaphorically, too wet, and in other places too dry, so the air has been filled all winter with the usual grumbles of discontented souls. And the winter of the church's healing ministry seems, over many a long year, to have become like winter in my garden —a hard and often fruitless search for satisfying answers, punctuated with only a few incomplete results. But now at last – physically in my garden, and spiritually in ministry – things are beginning to happen once more. In both these areas it might be said that the watery sun's rays seem at long last to throw their limp arms around me —when I turn my face towards the sky, the ground is warming and sprouting under my feet. The weeds have begun to grow in strength, and the lawns are spotted with long, tangled tufts that try to trip me as I feel my way down the clematis hedge this afternoon, as I work busily with a pair of secateurs. The more virulent varieties of clematis that decorate our home in Wales show little concern for their owners —they shoot and twine and bulge and lengthen! I informed our black Labrador of my decision: "This lot will have to be pruned back!" He quizzically jogged back and forth after me as I adopted a zigzag search pattern behind the gently murmuring ornamental firs and the swishing bamboo, until we found the wheelbarrow by skinning my shins on it! Then, armed with my trusty secateurs, we set off to bring order and restoration to the trellis. Well, that was the plan. With my mind still more tuned to pruning tumours than clematis, I cut and chopped and piled the surplus cuttings into the wheelbarrow by the armful, and flattened them down with my hands, wondering all the while why it was so easy. Half an hour and the barrow was not yet full, and I had not yet had to make the inevitable trip to the rubbish dump in the far bottom corner of the garden. What a wonderful wheelbarrow, I rejoiced, it never overflowed! Was this another kingdom miracle? But I should have known better, I should have remembered that I had seen this wonder before. I saw it a few years ago but then it was not clematis, it was while setting silver birch trees free from a throttling mass of ivy.

Suddenly the barrow's secret was out. I turned back to the clematis, catching my toe in a thick clump of grass and lost my balance. As I fell clumsily on my back on the soft green ground, I picked up the unmistakable sound of a black Labrador guide dog's scraping claws swiftly leaping out of a plastic wheelbarrow. As I rolled over to remonstrate with him, the bell on his play collar gave the game away —he sprang down, pulling mouthfuls of twisting vegetation out onto the lawn. He was engaged in his own programme of re-distribution, and it was fun —the lawn was now untidily strewn with clematis cuttings. His act of disobedience was going to set my plans back considerably. I collapsed with a sigh on the garden seat in the warming sun, to regain my motivation for gardening.

Summer comes around again to my garden and summer has come again to the preaching of the good news of the kingdom of God. This is the time of year for me to receive my usual seasonal instructions on pruning, and anything else that I can do to tidy up in the winter's wake. But there were dark forces working against me, at least in my horticultural efforts: The dog had apparently decided to enjoy these long pieces of green string with leaves on, together with the exciting whippy bits that flap around his ears when he shakes them vigorously from side to side. Here I was, trying to make a serious effort towards good stewardship and my guide dog was making hay while the sun shone!

I could only sit there and laugh at him, or perhaps with him, as he revelled in all the flourishing fresh growth of spring. Here was growth and abundance in my garden and, at the same time, growth and joy had come to the ministry of the miraculous healing of the sick and the injured. But there is certainly no spring without autumn and winter, no life without death. That is the way the Creator made it to be.

The green flushing leaves of summer turn brown and die, falling into the ground to fertilize it for the future. Fruit falls and rots so that seed can be released into its own little patch of fertile soil, acorns die to grow massive oak trees —and our Saviour died to release grace and truth into our world.

***

When Shirley developed lung cancer, we were all devastated. Being married to a member of our ministry team would mean that we had ready access to her and would come across her often in prayerful situations. It had taken her a little over a year to die. Leaving on one side for a moment the agony of her husband, the rest of us – hundreds of us, willingly, hopefully and lovingly – applied our shoulders to the wheel. We were determined that this would not happen. Prayer chains were formed; vigils were volunteered; sacraments became a regular part of her daily life. Bishops anointed her with oil, candles were lit in far-flung churches, intercessors heard from heaven that she would live, and prophets heard, apparently from the same source, that she would not.

As time went on, a number of her close friends, including myself when I could, lovingly and prayerfully threw at her everything we knew about the healing ministry. We trawled back through all the hours and hours of teaching we had received to find the clue.

We went to new lectures on root causes and pored over and over the tapes of old ones, praying and hoping for just one give-away sentence, one spark in the darkness that might reveal whatever might be the block, and release healing in her.

When we could not find the key to turn in her particular lock we fell into that deep trough of dark and commonly believed error that supposes there must be some unconfessed sin lurking from the past that God cannot work around. Failing that, we were even tempted at one point to reach for the blunt instrument of deliverance ministry, often the weapon of last resort for those who feel a sense of ministerial responsibility but are lost in it.

"O Jesus, answer us!" we shouted. But there was no response; no one answered. And we retreated into sacramental ministries and pseudo-prophetic guesswork of every kind.

What were we doing wrong? We wondered: 'Why could we not get God to fix this thing? Should we shout louder? Should we make bigger prayer chains? Should we have them all praying in waves? Surely he is Almighty God! Perhaps he is deep in thought or busy?' Perhaps he is sleeping, like Jesus in the storm-shaken boat, and has to be woken up somehow?

All we could do was pray more firmly, more strongly, more fiercely, more emotionally, but nothing we could see was stirring in heaven. Almighty God – our own God of grace and power and healing – appeared to have deserted her. Did he have a plan? Perhaps he had a secret script for all this, in which her dying played a vital and irreplaceable role? Could he not tell us what it was? What, I wondered, was the point of saving the world if he was only going to devise plans for us, beyond our understanding, necessitating our pain?

All our efforts were to no avail; her funeral was the break point. Now came the time, in the middle of all the bursting pain of emptiness and agonising loss, standing in that church at the centre of so much celebration of her life. Now came the time to climb down from this modern Christian pride box, which sustains all those who stand on it with all there is to know about healing theology. This was not a time to work it out any more; this was a time for recognising reality, abasement —and anguished confession.

"Where now is the Lord, the God of Elijah?" I yelled under my breath during the funeral service. Elijah had seen the fire of God come down with comparative ease and burn up his offering on Mount Carmel; where was he now? Elisha's heartfelt cry was an easy one to echo. Standing there in the middle of Shirley's funeral service, something about the Christian healing ministry dawned on me, not gently like some hard-sought revelation but with the brightness and crash of lightning. In quite a shocking contrast to my own ministry (and the ministry of the church as a whole, with only a few dazzling exceptions), Jesus found it easy to heal the sick in his day. Was this because he was also God? Well, the apostles found it comparatively easy and so did the elders and the early deacons and, it would seem, almost every Christian in the early church as well! In those far off days it would have been possible to recognise a Christian by the apparent ease by which the sick around them were healed. The disciples of Jesus were known to lay their hands on the sick, who then became well again.

But I was now feeling that this was not true for me! Come to think of it, this was not the experience for most other Christians I knew, either! The Spirit of Christ worked at will in the early church, and since then there had been some miracles —but now, I wondered, where was the love and the fairness in singling out a few? Has God ceased to heal? Had all that teaching I had received over the years been wasted? Had I missed some important issue here? Was there something badly wrong in me that God found it impossible to work through? But I thought I had inherited at Calvary, like every other Christian, a robe of righteousness to cover my filthiness; why can God not work through me? If not through me, then why could he not have worked through some speck of holiness in all the people and their tons of prayer that had boomed upwards, all the tears, all the compassion, all the weight in a hundred hearts? There must have been a chink of the righteousness of Christ in all that somewhere. If he had really wanted to, I felt certain he could have found a way.

Such was the boiling feeling in my raging heart —at least, during Shirley's funeral service. Nothing of this could be spoken out; times like these are too full of other people's pain and deep need of God. It would be best if any angry soul on the end of a packed church pew were to keep his own counsel.

***

But those same outraged feelings, in content though not in depth, never left me. "Dear God," I begged over my sandwiches one busy conference lunchtime a while later, "the way we do it in the church just simply doesn't seem to work very well at all. I have learned so much over my years of working with you and yet I seem to know nothing. When the chips are down, there is absolutely nothing the church can do about it but deliver a lot of platitudes, and sound very spiritual in the process. I have seen your glorious hand in healing many a spiritual or emotional problem, but the need for you to get involved again in physical illness is nothing short of staggering! The world is brimming over with sickness of every kind imaginable; we are crying out for you to be like you used to be. You used to do it, less and less as the years have rolled on since Jesus, but now it is all so rare! Now all we can do is wonder: Why not? Now we spend all our time trying to work out theological sounding excuses for failure. Of course we cannot call it your failure because you are omnipotent and omniscient and therefore you cannot fail. But it seems as though you failed Shirley and thousands like her —and the hundreds of us who begged you to move. The church has also taught us that you never change, yet you surely seem to. There was a day when you healed everyone who asked Jesus and now you do not. They tell us that you are unconditional love, and yet you heal one or two and not the majority. Is that love? You say that your yoke is light, but you seem to let us down all the time! The one simple, sought after gift that Jesus gave away so readily now causes more pain and doubt and argument about you than anything else I know. So show me your glory! The question I have for you is this: as the church does not know how to do it like you did it, how did you do it, and how did you teach it so effectively? What did you teach them who followed you? What, for the sake of the glory of Christ, have we lost?"

For half an hour I ranted and raved like this and beat on the gates of heaven. By the end of that lunch break, my healing ministry as I knew it had died. Deep down in the bottom of things, too deep even to admit it fully even to myself, it died. No one even suspected it except me and God and a few chosen friends, but everything I had learned from the church over ten years of full time healing ministry slipped, silently, into the grave.

In the same way that a new seed lies on the ground, encased in the rotting remains of a once glorious fruit, it was then, amazingly and beyond comprehension, that the light of Christ began to flood the darkness. I did not have long to wait.

Chapter Two

FALLING INTO THE MIRACULOUS LIFE

The results of that small but outrageous prayer turned out to be something so huge and so different that they have been shaking those who pray for the sick ever since with disease-shattering simplicity.

It was not long before the seed began to germinate. In a second teaching session that very afternoon, after the sandwiches and the prayer of surrender, we were pleasantly surprised to find every seat taken. Yet more expectant folk came in and sat on the floor along the aisles and across the back of the platform behind me. The place was packed. There must have been half as many again as the official capacity of the room. It was great to see them all but I could not help thinking 'What is going on, here?'

The guitar player had not turned up to lead us in singing, so we said one psalm together as a gathering act of worship and then, with all my courage ebbing away and out through the toes of my boots, I took a deep breath and asked the simple question of the audience, "Who needs a miracle in their life this afternoon?" The room seemed filled with waving hands, barley stalks in a field white for harvest.

At first I still felt bold, but soon became very scared. I checked with myself that I knew exactly where the door was in case I needed a fast exit. If God did not turn up at this point, my ministry would be well and truly ruined! Well, that would not be much of a loss, I managed to smile to myself, it does not work very well, anyway.

I began to preach the good news of Jesus Christ by reminding them that he healed everyone who asked him —everyone, that is, with a modicum of expectant faith, and he repeatedly told us that he could only do what the Father was doing. The only people I could find in the New Testament who did not receive healing were those who did not ask Jesus for it. I drew the simple conclusion from these facts that God's will must be to see healed all who come to Jesus for restoration.

It was God himself who took the opportunity to demonstrate his grace at that point, I had no more to say to them and little to do with what followed. There was an agonising silence for what seemed like an hour, but was probably only the audience shock that lasted a few seconds. It was almost as if they had never been spoken to like that before!

Then, to coin a phrase, all heaven let loose. Skin complaints were cleared up, chronic pain disappeared, a fused spine became flexible, pain free and pliable. One lady stood without sticks for the first time in twenty years. Another lady with a muscle wasting disease stopped shaking; one toothache died away and one man's damaged knee ligaments were completely restored so that he was able to return to work the following Monday morning after spending three months on sick leave.

One person walking past the conference room outside the building received healing for a bad back, without any prayer at all, and two ladies were freed from arthritic knees quite spontaneously while sitting next to each other watching it all. That was the first time we saw what we came to know as 'shadow healing', a feature of the kingdom which I shall come back to.

Fearful? Frightening? To be avoided at all cost? Did the people in that room think so? They were being healed. If we truly have the Spirit of Christ within, how can we do anything but rejoice with them? Why should this sort of thing be happening? Well, mankind is as nothing compared with God. But with him, working in tandem with him, we can be like pearls of great value; we can reflect something of Jesus; we are heirs of eternal life and beneficiaries of his will. We were made to rise above death forever, and before then to live this life in wholeness until we arrive in heaven! Standing on the lecture platform that afternoon, I saw all this.

The journey home from that conference should normally be about an hour and a half by road. It felt as though it took five minutes; we flew. What had happened? Why, after all these years of hard, dead-horse-flogging, theorising and excuse making, sacrificial, heartbreaking praying for the sick, had it suddenly become comparatively easy? What had we done? If God does not change then we must have done. But how?

On the trip home that evening we made long lists in the car of everyone we had prayed for and those of them who had seen a noticeable improvement before the afternoon was out. Somewhere in excess of a third of all those waving hands had recognised improvement in their various conditions. Added to those, of course, would be the illnesses that cannot be measured without medical intervention and those that were to take a while longer to mend. We were elated. This sort of level of answered prayer had not been seen for a number of years as far as we were aware, and here it was again.

Hundreds of healing services and numerous teaching schools and conferences around the world, and it goes on. The number of the sick and the injured able to receive relief and restoration has increased considerably since then. Everywhere the good news of Jesus is fully preached, the miracles confirm it.

And as for Shirley's husband? I suggested to him, not long after that first fruitful conference talk, that he might be angry in his humanity that all this had not happened eighteen months earlier. There could have been, I suggested, a chance that Shirley might still be alive. But, so full of wisdom as he always is, he gently explained to me that he sees God's desire to heal to be rather like penicillin. It has existed since the beginning of time but we have only recently discovered it. There is no future in remorse for the millions that could have been saved by it before its discovery —we simply rejoice that we have found it at last!

Half a dozen years and thousands of healing miracles later, we know what happened that day. We were prepared to throw away all our concepts about a healing God and take a giant step of trust into the relatively unknown.

As for 'shadow' healing...? This must surely be one of the greatest delights of this kingdom ministry. This particular type of miracle has gained its name from the record of Peter walking to the Temple one day. People were bringing the sick into the streets on beds and mats and laying them on the pavements, so that at least Peter's shadow might fall on some of them as he passed by. They were all healed. There was no prayer recorded here, and Jesus had ascended to heaven a while earlier. Yet they were all healed.

So – as we find frequently occurring during the preaching of the good news of Jesus – many are healed quite spontaneously without any prayer being said for them. It is not unusual to see damaged neck vertebrae restored, bent and battered fingers straightened, arthritic hands renewed, asthma disappearing, withered hands rebuilt, hearing given and skin complaints vanishing away without any recourse to ministry. No one prays, the hearers are simply washed with the truth about Jesus in his kingdom, the living word of God.

Why should this shadow healing be one of the greatest delights of healing ministry? Because when spontaneous healing breaks out there cannot be any doubt at all in anyone's mind as to who is doing the work. When working miracles in the kingdom, there is no need to repeatedly explain who is doing the healing – the minister or Christ – the truth is being amply demonstrated to everyone by the Holy Spirit, without any explanation.

Only two months before the time of writing this, and almost six years after that first dramatic conference encounter with our healing God, we were invited to give a most memorable lecture on living in the kingdom; I write the word 'memorable' because some of these teaching days stand out more than others in my memory, either for the things that go wrong or for the things that go right! This one was plagued by, of all things in this modern day and age, technological problems. Microphones, computers and electricity were in chaos.

The power supply was at best intermittent from the moment we arrived at the church, and finally it gave up the ghost altogether about half way through the time of worship that began the day. However, it all soon settled down, picked up again and went well enough, and Almighty God blessed us greatly with a sense of his presence and with those signs and wonders which quietly and reliably prove the truth of full kingdom preaching. Quietly and reliably? Yes, that is the way of things when we begin to walk on the water of the kingdom of God.

A short while after that session of kingdom teaching, sitting opposite me across the kitchen table at The Well, our headquarters in south Wales, was a lady who had attended the talk two months earlier and had driven a long way to ask a question. She is a greatly gifted Christian devotional writer and leader of retreats.

"Mike," she said to me over her coffee cup, "what's going on?"

I was intrigued. "Tell me more, I'm all ears!"

She took a large swallow and set her mug down on the table, leaned back in her chair and began to tell her tale. She did not realise it then, but she was wanting to talk about shadow healing.

"Since that lecture I have led two retreats," she explained. "Now, at some point during my time with people on these occasions, leading them in quiet meditation, people have been getting healed of all sorts of things. They are supposed to walk out thoughtfully and they go out dancing!"

"Yes?" I tried with a grin to provoke her to go on, but she needed little encouragement to share this exciting news.

"Well, I don't do anything! I'm not praying with them, I'm not specifically mentioning healing grace or trying to pray in a healing way —it just happens!"

She explained again that she would normally expect people to leave the retreat venue at the end of their time together with her in a contemplative mood, but some go out dancing and chatting with joy.

"So here's my question," she said again, "what's going on?"

"Well," I teased her, "I do believe you're becoming a kingdom walker!" Then we talked together for a while, chewing over the exciting news about shadow healing in the kingdom.

But things did not end there. She announced, as she got ready to leave, that her ankle was giving her not a little trouble. There did not seem anything particularly wrong but she had experienced a continuous sensation of pins and needles for some weeks and the ankle was very weak and threatened to turn over whenever she put her weight on it.

"May I have some prayer ministry before I go?" she asked.

Five minutes and she was walking normally. The horrid needling sensation had completely vanished and the ankle was as strong as the other.

"This is quite strange!" she told us as we prayed. "It's as though someone is inside the skin, rebuilding the bones and ligaments and muscles and putting everything in order!"

Of course we are thrilled with her as she skips out to her car, but that sort of thing is nowadays all in a day's work, really.

One week later I had a note from her.

Dear Mike,

Thank you for giving up a morning to talk to me about my experiences of spontaneous healing whilst leading meditational worship. It was very helpful to talk with you and I continue to feel a strong sense that the Lord desires me to develop this ministry that He has so richly gifted me with.

The amazing experiences continue ... and I'd like to share one with you.

A very dear friend of mine has suffered for many years. As part of this, regular routine scans are a feature of her life. She had one last week and was stunned to find that the consultant wanted to operate immediately. The scan had revealed a very large and potentially life threatening [possibly malignant] tumour, and her husband was gently counselled that this was very unlikely to have a good outcome —he was advised to prepare for the worst.

She was admitted to hospital the following day. Her husband called up several people and asked them to pray, including me.

I began along the usual lines of 'Please give wisdom and skill to the surgeons, peace to my friend, etc., etc....' All the stuff that we are inclined to pray at these times. Then I felt a strong sense of being drawn to pray in a radically different way and I felt physically held in prayer for what turned out to be a long, long time —well over an hour.

I recalled what I had heard from and witnessed in you ... and I completely changed the focus of my prayers ... beginning firstly with a time of real praise to Jesus, and then daring to pray for the complete shrinking and disappearance of the tumour and a complete restoration of healthy functioning to all her organs.

I'm sure you can guess where this is leading, though the thought of it still bowls me over. When the surgeon operated on her, to his amazement, he was completely unable to find any evidence of the tumour! The surgeon is in total disbelief, and wanting to do a second scan today to double check. Her husband is in awe-struck shock ... and I'm pretty bowled over too. Wonderful! Amazing! Radical healing of the order that challenges all our preconceptions! How can I not allow God to develop this ministry....

I am aware that I was one of many committed Christians praying for her, but I do wonder how many others prayed in such a radical way. Either way, I feel immensely drawn to allow God to develop this work in me, and I am sure that I will be applying to attend your Kingdom Healing programme later this year.

All this had happened to her in a remarkably short space of time, and all because she had understood how to take the first tiny step towards the promised land of the kingdom of God. She was learning the basics of her role in miraculous kingdom living.

The working of miracles is not anything to be proud of, or to boast about, but it is something that can be taught and shared to the glory of Christ. It is not that I have been especially anointed at some special personal time to work miracles; the whole church worldwide was anointed this way at Pentecost so that the world could enjoy the inheritance of Calvary. If 'Christian' is a label, then 'disciple' is a way of life. If only we disciples could open the door to the kingdom again, so that the children of God could really benefit from their promised inheritance!

But, from a theological point of view, we have to get into the right place to start and we are far from it. Over the intervening centuries since Jesus' earthly ministry, the slowly thickening and suffocating mist of religious philosophy that has kept the suffering from knowing kingdom realities has been allowed to develop and over-run so much that we can only catch glimpses here and there of the trellis that supported early Church mission so miraculously.

So what does it mean to be a kingdom walker? What is such a person? And how on earth do we set out to achieve such a thing?

The first step to take is in humility; we begin by recognising that most stages of Christian growth are not arrival lounges but departure platforms. Wherever we might understand ourselves to be, the place on which we stand is only a launch pad. The holy ground on which Moses stood in front of the burning bush was not to be a bolt-hole for him, a place to hide himself in the warmth and security of the everlasting arms: it was the end of a diving board from which he would be launched into great adventures. Wherever we might be in our Christian walk, we will never move onwards if we are not open to the idea of moving.

The initial difficulty in understanding kingdom walking is this: We tend to believe that the place in which we stand as Christians is the right place for us. But there is a mighty leap ahead which is quite awesome in the width of its chasm. It is relatively unknown but is not to be underestimated. Many Christians will have made a leap of that size in joining a church in the first place. Many others will have made such a leap in inviting Christ to be the Lord and Saviour of their lives. Some streams of spirituality in the church demand yet other great steps, which are not what we are considering here. This is the place, though, to declare the exciting truth that becoming a kingdom walker, after the model of the early Christians, as seen throughout the New Testament, is probably going to demand a massive re-think. We are told to, "Repent, for the kingdom of heaven is near" —and repenting requires that we think again. So, to begin our journey into the miraculous life, we might dwell for a while on the fact that a re-think is needed.

It is important, in the early stages of comprehension, to develop a sense of what it means to live in the kingdom. This is not simply about living a good, productive and Christian life by any usually accepted measures —it is about learning to walk in harness with God.

Anyone who has had, as I did, the undoubted privilege of living on a tidal estuary will cherish many memory pictures —joyful slices of youth. One of these, one which has deeply affected my understanding of what it means to become a kingdom walker, is a brightly coloured picture of rows of beached sailing boats along a sea-weedy yacht club foreshore line, with stays slapping gently against angled masts in the breeze. Here are rolling green and wooded hillsides sloping down to blue waters, and the tiny harbour, with vessels of all shapes, sizes and colours resting at anchor. Even now, in my mind's eye, I can count the trees along the shoreline and see the wing tips of the swans as they beat the water: a long line astern of dazzling white bodies and stretched white necks, lifting and taking off in the evening light. They often came slapping down the quiet river towards the sea, one behind the other, a double row of rippling pools streaming back from their wing tips, like the oar dips of an eight-man rowing team, as their feathers touch the still evening water.

Chapter Three

A QUESTION OF ATTITUDE

There was a different version of my original estuary memory given to me some while ago, while I was praying to understand the size – and the effect – of making the leap I mentioned earlier, the leap that I took from ordinary Christian churchgoing to becoming a 'kingdom walker' —the way of discipleship as it seems to have been in the New Testament.

To let one's mind imagine the earliest days of the Christian church is to watch its members, as well as its leaders, being quite used to the idea of preaching the kingdom of God as a piece of good news; as they did this, the Holy Spirit frequently worked signs and wonders to demonstrate the truth and reality of what they were saying. Miracles, the pastoral and restorative work of the Holy Spirit, happened on a daily basis with them.

Today's preachers all believe they speak of the kingdom, yet it may be observed that a consequential free flow of miracles is no longer the norm. Some claim that the supernatural Christian life is all over anyway, while others present the kingdom as a somewhat thin and watered-down version of what is to come. Still others blame God for what might seem like his apparent reluctance, suggesting that his will differs from the reliable will that Jesus displayed according to the Gospels, while yet others blame supplicants for having too many blockages, hurdles too high to climb over. All this modern thick cobweb of religious philosophy is such an exhausting minefield of error to wade through —even the very thought of it is confusing! It did no good debating intellectually the whys and wherefores of all this: Does he still do it or not? Why does he do it for some and not others? What do I say when he does not do it? I did not want any part of such argument, I only ever wanted to give freely the grace and the power of the message of the cross to those who suffer. I have no real wish to contend or deliberate such things, but a real desire to see healing. Indeed, most of us do very much want to see healing, but, for the majority, the motivation is to lessen suffering, prolong life, and avoid the pain and distress of illness. All these are wholly understandable emotions, but they have the tendency of sending us off in search of yet another form of 'medicine' that might succeed where others might have failed us. This then in turn reduces Christian healing prayer ministry to being just another optional type of alternative or complementary medical treatment.

One can tell when the church has lost the original vision and designated healing as an optional type of ministry. It is either when it becomes desperate to include the medically trained in its ranks or allows itself the luxury of sidelining the whole business at the first sign of its becoming uncomfortable or incomprehensible. But divine healing was not meant to be a complementary medicine requiring scientific justification, nor an incomprehensible option to be dispensed with. It is a sign of the apostolic, it is the normal and everyday outworking of the preaching of the good news of the message of the cross in its fullness.

I fondly remember one set of elderly parents approaching me at the end of a healing service, asking, "Do you remember our daughter, Megan?"

"I'm sorry," I had to say, "please forgive me, there have been so many...."

"You prayed with us about her a week ago," the mother went on. "She had a massive stroke three weeks ago and was in intensive care?"

I must have been looking a little less blank because she continued, in her brimming-over joy.

"She lost all her speech and hearing. They said the stroke had scrambled her brain. She was completely paralysed except she could move her eyelids, and must have had some sight as she was looking vaguely about the place as if she was hunting for something she did not understand. Well, she's out of intensive care inside a week, since we prayed together. Her sight and her speech and hearing are completely restored and her mind is exactly as it was. She has about eighty per cent mobility already and the rest is coming on just fine! They say she should be home from hospital by the end of this week!"

I grinned uncontrollably and cried a great deal with them. I was overcome with the desire to bottle that mother's tears and her voice —not the words or the water, but the emotion within them. I longed to break open the bottle in front of so many who doubt, debate and fear the miraculous. Just for one weak, unforgiving and sinful moment I would have given anything to wave that bottle under the noses of all those who have no desire to take a step into this glorious kingdom for the sake of their Saviour. For a fleeting moment I imagined myself asking them, 'Where is your compassion? Can you not take a risk for such mothers as this?' But it is not for me to usurp the role of prompter. That belongs rightly to the Holy Spirit.

But I do admit that I am coming at healing from a slightly different angle than many do. Anger plays its part: anger against what the enemy of our souls has done. Adam and Eve made a bad mistake, and we all pay the price for it. Adam was given authority over the whole earth and everything in it, but he gave it away to Satan. However, God the Father, in his forgiving grace, sent Jesus the Son to rescue us from the wiles of the devil, and hand that delegated authority back to us, where it should rightly have been all along had it not been for the Fall.

So we are left with two sides of a coin, so to speak. We have the total and painful mess, as a result of Adam's disobedience, and we have the antidote of the cross with which to defeat it. I am left with anger at Satan for causing so much suffering in the world, though we unwittingly allowed it in the first place, and I feel so sad for those who fall into pain and difficulty as a result.

On the other hand I owe it to Jesus, after all he has done for me, to take the fullest possible advantage of Calvary, to do my utmost to ensure that not one little drop of that blessed sacrifice is ever wasted. He gave us his cross and the kingdom, and the instructions needed to use it.

I suppose that confusion over this kingdom business is hardly surprising. Jesus teaches us that we will only be able to see the kingdom if we approach it in a child-like manner. There must be a simplicity of spirit. That is where my estuary vision comes in. It can help us to see the difference between, on the one hand, the historical ministry of the church in the area of healing and, on the other, the wonderful gift of simple kingdom living and its consequences!

I remember the vision as if it were given yesterday. If I lean back and shut my eyes, I am standing knee-deep in the cool waters of an estuary, some three feet from the bank, roasting in the afternoon heat on my back and the reflecting rays of the sun coming off the surface of the water onto my arms and face. I fight a sense of sinking in my heart as I allow my gaze to drift up and down the river bank in front of me; all away to my left and down to my right there are plants wilting and dying in the direct glare of the sun, the parched heat and the dry soil. So near and yet so far— rows and rows of plants only a few inches from the water's edge and yet drying out and dying out in the heat of the day. And so it is to have compassion for the sick and injured among us.

I must minister to them in the only way I know how. I bend down, scooping my cupped hands up from between my knees and splashing the nearest plants with the healing, cooling water they need in order to survive. I seem to do this a hundred, if not a thousand times, while my back seems as if it is breaking and I am simply not satisfied with the results. When, eventually, my tears of exasperation begin to flow down and mix themselves with the handfuls of water, the nearest plants develop darker brown earth around them and in time, some – not many – seem to recover slightly.

I stand up to stretch my muscles, aching from the work, and wipe my sleeve across my streaming forehead. I glance up and down the bank again at the acres of suffering plants, and return to my labours.

Retrieving my watch from my pocket, I look at it quickly. Another two hours or so and I can go home, secure in the knowledge that I have done my best for another day. I swallow down the thought that I will most likely have failed many more plants than I will be able to rescue, but then how can I be expected to do everything around here? After all, I am only one among many. I cannot see any other colleagues from my spot in the river but I am sure they must be around somewhere! As far as I can see, I am doing the job aright. I am metaphorically standing in the river of God's saving grace and doing my little bit to pastor, through that grace, the ones nearest to me. This is all a man can do. Anyway, I am taught to be humble —I must not assume in any way that the success of the kingdom or its ministry depends on me!

In a little while I straighten up again, stretching my shoulders backwards to ease the muscle stiffness in them. But who comes here? From away to my right through the heat haze emerges a rider, a shimmering white horse clopping along the riverside path towards me. I will use his coming to wait and rest on the off chance of some conversation.

Hoof beat by hoof beat he slowly approaches, and then, as he reaches me, he reins in his horse and leans slowly forward, face turned towards me and forearms resting on the pommel. The broad brim of his hat obscures much of his face in shadow.

"Good afternoon, sir," I offer.

"May I ask what you are doing?" he enquires of me.

"I was walking along here this morning," I told him, "and caught sight of all these lovely plants and flowers up and down the river bank. They were doing very badly in the heat of the day. They were suffering and dying, and yet all they were doing was just being here! I wanted to help so I climbed into the river and began to scoop water. I have no bucket or hose, only my hands. I suppose that's alright because it's the water that does the refreshing, not me! But now my back is getting the better of me so I shall stop soon and go home for a rest!"

Without taking his eyes off me for a moment he raises himself upright again in the saddle and says, "Follow me!"

"Who are you?" I ask him in turn. I am tired and hot and dirty and I want to go home. If I am going to follow someone at this end point of such a dusty and exhausting day, heaven only knows where, I would need to know what I am going to let myself in for.

The rider waves a hand along the far estuary bank, all the way along in one direction and back along the near bank. "All this is mine." He is smiling fondly at the whole vista of browns and greens and blues in front of him when he says this. "The river is mine and the ground to either side is mine. Where the estuary comes from is mine and where it flows into the sea is mine. The air above it is mine and the plants are mine. Follow me and I will show you something."

So I do. It seems uncomfortable to be carried along like this; I was right to do what I had been doing, I was right to be where I was and now it is right to go home. But I take a step of faith. This is against my better judgement but I take the step, nevertheless. His words seem to want to direct my path.

I climb and slip unsteadily back up the bank and roll down my trouser legs. I slip my socks and shoes on again as he applies his heels and the white horse sets off at a walking pace, the rider never looking back to see if I am following, but I am. And so we go on for a little while, no one speaking. I am finding strength and support in the sweltering heat by pacing my footsteps in the rhythm of the horses' hooves. Straight on we go for over a mile, turning to the right as we follow the line of the river around a wide bend to a place where it widens out even further, between the wooded hillsides that hold a boathouse at their feet.

"There," he points out to me, "in that boathouse is a gift for you. You have worked hard on my river and you have worked well with my flowers, but now I have a reward for you. Enjoy it and you will learn something."

Intrigued, I climb down the wooded slope until I reach the boat shed door, left unlocked and lightly ajar in its own welcome. Inside is a sight that takes my breath away. Lying there quietly, waiting for me, is the sleekest and most beautiful speedboat I have ever seen. It has two mighty motors mounted on its stern, and the painter is cast loose in readiness for me. I turn to wave my thanks to the rider, but of course he is gone.

The main boat shed doors are lying open onto the water. Both engines roar and leap into life at my touch. The bow lifts to the wooded banks on the other side, and the stern sinks as the propeller blades bite deep.

Managing to stay upright under the forces of acceleration, I throw the tiller to one side and we are away up river, white water boiling behind me, wind playing with my hair and keeping my face cool as the evening sun burns down. We roar very quickly up river until it seems right to turn the boat around. The engines soften and the bow turns, only to rise again towards the sky as I let the engines have their freedom. Soon we are racing past the boat shed again on our way downstream, and all thoughts of strain and stress are gone. Anxiety has left me, and my aching shoulders are beginning to recover strength after the day's toil. All is well. I open the throttles as far as they will go — this is the stuff that any child's adventure is made of!

As the way ahead appears empty, safe and clear for a moment, I turn around to look behind, and thrill with the sight of it. The blue-white waves, one issuing from either side of the stern, broaden and widen out behind me as I go, until, a long way behind me they reach the bank. This wall of water is quite high enough to fling itself far up the dry earth bank —and the deluge completely swamps every plant, every struggling and suffering flower and weed alike, almost up as high as the rider's footpath, and certainly for the entire length of the river. To complete my joy for them all, the other wave soaks and nearly drowns the opposite bank to exactly the same extent.

And how much effort have I put in now to saving the plants? None at all. All I have done is enjoy myself in taking the fullest advantage of the gift of the boat and access to the river. So then it begins to dawn on me — effective ministry will never be a function of how hard I work or how cleverly I work, it will be the fallout of my living in, and enjoying to the full, the kingdom. The realisation of this truth is stunning — I have never even heard a whisper of it before.

I cut the engines and we glide gently to a halt in the quiet of the river. There is no sign of the rider anywhere along either bank, but I can only fall to my knees in the bottom of the boat and thank him for this revelation. I would never have imagined that I could have watered the banks in that dramatically effective way. He has shown me the gift of his cross and given me access to, and authority in, the kingdom. He has taught me that all I need to do is to thank him and praise him, and enjoy my kingdom living, and the plants around me will in their turn receive in my wake.

"But all this is too easy!" I shout towards the wooded river bank in the hope that he might hear me, but there is no answer. His silence seems like the deep and contented acceptance of heaven.

The lesson of the estuary vision is clear – the regular and consistent healing of the sick is not best achieved through a particular methodology, nor by choice of ritual, nor by deeds and actions, nor even necessarily by petition prayer. It will not have escaped the reader's attention that consistent results by any of these means is nothing short of grinding hard work, if indeed such a successful ministry is possible at all! And I have been shown something that I badly needed to know before any healing ministry could really work through me to any sizeable and reliable degree. I have seen that divine healing is not a ministry after all, it is the natural outworking of an everyday disciple. It is the natural kingdom dynamic that results from the bold and full preaching of the good news of the cross. If anything, we should be starting to think of it not as a subject in its own right but as part of the ministry of the word.

Putting it another way, messing about in the river up to my knees is a picture of a minister trying his best to disseminate grace. Driving up and down in the speedboat is a picture of a disciple enjoying his true kingdom role, that of proclamation of the cross at the heart of that kingdom. The kingdom walker is a disciple who simply enjoys praising and giving thanks for all that Jesus has done, and is living in the kingdom to the utmost —and people receive healing in his wake. This thought must surely bring joy to any serious Christian.

The revealed secret of this kingdom living is interlaced throughout the structure of the New Testament. It is neither exclusively mine nor my colleagues' or anyone else's; it belongs to each one of us who is called to partake of it. We are strongly warned not to think of it as some private revelation, in case we are consequently stripped of its joy.

So, through the estuary vision, the scene is set. The beginning of my understanding about the kingdom, and most importantly my relationship with it, had arrived. I have heard it said sometimes that even if there were no rights or wrongs assumed about the way we do any kind of ministry, the church, created by Jesus to further the work of the kingdom of God, could always be judged by the extent to which we are successful in advancing that kingdom.

But I can now see that this idea comes from a misunderstanding of what is meant by the 'kingdom of God'. The kingdom itself is not something to be 'furthered' or 'built on' by our efforts. It is something which we are asked to realise as being here already, in the life and work of Jesus. It is something that we who believe in Christ should not be actively trying to grow and stretch and give away, as I had been trying to do in the river up to my knees. It is something to inherit and enter into. The role of the church, in these matters, is not to persuade the world how it might be a better place than it is at present, but to draw a curtain aside from it, to reveal something that is already here.

Chapter Four

STANDING AT THE WATER'S EDGE

Chewing over joyful slices of my youth, I recall tidal estuaries and dark green wooded hillsides, whose dark overhanging frowns reflect in the water along the river banks; it is such a pleasing thing to revisit those scenes when time allows.

I go back to that place – not only the memory, but the actual place of memory – as often as I can. Along the edge of the estuary, as it used to be, there is a narrow, twisting lane, a wall a few feet from my left elbow beyond which is a sheer drop to the water. If I step to the right along that lane and reach out my hand I touch the front wall of a row of quiet, blossom covered, pretty terraced thatched cottages, all fair dwellings for flocks of swifts and swallows – holiday homes these days for the housemartins and the well-heeled from the city.

I can only marvel at my guide dog. He always marches steadfastly along, watching to left and right, at the same time as looking ahead in case of any obstacle along the way. He is on his best guiding form at moments like this, a feat deserving particular mention and high praise as the magnetic smell of the river must invade every nerve. Is he particularly alert because of the tricky terrain or does he search every possibility for an escape passage down to the river?

The lane suddenly slopes alarmingly downwards and comes to an abrupt end. At low tide I would expect the tarmac to peter out on the mud and gravel foreshore further down, but the last time we were there the evening high tide was full, and my dog had stopped at the water's softly slapping edge.

I dropped the harness to signal the end of his time of duty and he took three steps forward to the extent of his lead, till the water reached his stomach and chest. There he stopped, sideways on and staring straight at me, eyebrows raised in an unspoken question. As easily as one senses someone else's eyes boring into one's back, I had learned to sense the flickering of his eyebrows in my soul.

We stood there for a while, staring at each other and realising mountains of differing feelings. This was hard for him, so hard! All his natural Labrador nature, generations of breeding and genes passing down the line, all his upbringing, screamed at him to let go, to throw himself into play, to charge off into the waiting adventure, full of silver spray and deep dark green water.

But he could not move. He was locked where he was. He was still wearing his guiding harness and he was fully aware of it. All his nature shouts at him to go, and all his training tells him he should stay put, in control —watchful, commanding, mature, sensible, full of self-confidence and authority.

His questioning eyebrows were demanding a decision from me. If I slipped his harness he would be in the middle of the estuary before I could blink. If I called him he would be at my side even quicker. He was wrestling inside. His mind must have been full of turmoil but he stood his ground.

Was it, I found myself wondering, much the same sensation for those priests who, under Joshua's command, stood looking at the Jordan in full spate and possibly doubting their own sanity? God had already told them that he had given Jericho on the other side into their hands; he had already made his intentions quite clear. They approached the flooding river with the Ark on their backs, containing the Ten Commandments, the piece of manna and the rod of Aaron that had budded; everything they knew about God was carried on their backs. Everything my guide dog knows about guiding, his harness and how to handle it, lives on his back.

I wondered if, in the same way that the dog was fighting himself at that moment, so too did those priests fight themselves inside. One wrong move on their part, one careless slip, and everything they stood for, everything they knew and believed about God, would be lost. They would not be able to control the situation; it would be a total, foot-slipping disaster, carried away by the flood. But they knew what to do. They knew how to overcome. They had heard God. One step forward from the first priest and the waters would apparently part for them. Dry land and Jericho and the promised land lay ahead, because one giant step of faith would be behind them. In the natural world of human common sense, they must have been thinking this one simple move to be indescribably foolish, but hindsight and memory of that event would give glory to God. They crossed into the middle of the river Jordan on dry ground.

It begins to dawn on me that this is exactly my experience. To become a kingdom walker, to walk naturally up and down in the promised land, to see the rightful beneficiaries inherit the promises, to see regular and consistent miraculous wall tumbling, all this requires just one step, a dangerous step, an apparently foolish step, but a step of obedience that changes everything. This is how we begin to become walkers in the kingdom of God. We honestly take stock of our prayer experiences with God. We recognise that persuading him to heal the sick and the injured supernaturally bears no resemblance to the atmosphere of released freedom depicted in that surfing speedboat on the river, nor the flow of ministry seen in the early church.

Anything more than passing intercession for the sick is much more like the picture of standing knee deep in the river, shovelling the badly needed water, a handful at a time, onto the nearest plants. It is hard work, if it is to be faithful and consistent, and it achieves, if truth be recognised, remarkably little.

Of course we would find it difficult admitting to that, being Christians. Because we know that God is love and God is good we have to stay in forgetful denial about all those helpless and hopeless times of prayer, those half-hearted prayers thrown heavenward which may help, or may just help things not to get any worse!

If we stand still long enough to survey realistically the whole scene of sickness and injury around us, we might soon find ourselves tumbling into depression at the sight of such volumes of suffering. At the end of any prayer time we look at our watch and go home, believing maybe that we have done our bit. Prayer, we tell ourselves, is all we can do about anything, really. The death of the remaining plants, the unresolved suffering of the sick, we wash away from our minds, a clever piece of social denial, so that we can get on with life. But we know this is a bad place to be!

There is a restlessness about all this in the depths of the Christian spirit. Somehow we instinctively know that this is not how it should be. And we are right!

Back at the estuary's edge, I moved on. I stood a moment longer beside the lapping water with my guide dog, wondering what the rich man at his banqueting table in the Bible story must have thought of the poor beggar, sitting with his sores at the gate, waiting and hoping for bread. I guess he must have only thought of this sick beggar as part of the landscape, really, if he saw him at all. He must have gone virtually unnoticed most of the time, as the rich man went in and out of his house. I can scarcely bear to think what afterlife of hell must be like for the rich man in Jesus' story. How can a Christian like me possibly allow the sick to remain part of the landscape or ignored, as the rich man did to Lazarus? If I have, as I like to believe, received the Spirit of Christ, then that Spirit must be the agent that burns away and changes my being so that I can begin to gain the mind of Christ.

We know from the Gospels that Jesus had compassion for the sick and longed to see the kingdom revealed to their sickness. If only the complacent rich man had the advantage of the Spirit of Christ!

Even so, praying for people is hard work. Most often we ask, we beg, we cajole, we promise, we make deals with God, and we sometimes even cry out before we give up. When we do give up we quieten our conscience with such human imaginings as God having other plans for the sick person, or that death is the great healer anyway, or that pain is God's way of purifying the soul. If such excuses do not come naturally to our theologies, then we shrug our shoulders over the next sick person and say to ourselves something like: 'Perhaps he really didn't want to be healed after all', or 'Perhaps, like prison, he takes some comfort in his illness. If it isn't this that is killing him, then perhaps he has some great unrepented sin that God cannot forgive him for and therefore cannot heal because of its blocking effect.'

We could of course say only one prayer, tell ourselves that the responsibility is God's now, and move on and away to other things. When it is time to give up the hard work of healing prayer, we silently blame the awfulness of life, and take our aching prayer knees home. We have a God who we know hears our prayers and loves us but in the matter of healing the sick, we start to doubt whether he is consistent and reliable. As Christians we cannot ever admit to this aloud but that is sometimes what our experience seems to tell us, and questions and doubts come: I know that God is no preferer of persons, but he sometimes heals my neighbour and not me! God, we say, is in control, and then a prayed for friend dies in a traffic accident. Why so? What sort of a deity would heal one stroke victim and not another? What sort of loving God could not afford an angel to protect a motor car? We may avoid all these nagging doubts and questions, slipping into the easy spiritual denial of calling it all 'mystery'.

But wait! Whatever happened to Jesus? The Jesus of Matthew, Mark, Luke and John never behaved in that way. He may not have healed everybody, but he most certainly did heal everyone who came to him and asked him. He never said 'No.' He never told anyone to wait. No sick person was ever commanded to sort their own lives out first before they could receive healing. He never gave up half way through. He never discerned the Father's will in matters of healing to be anything other than 'Yes' and 'Amen'. He said that he only did and said what he saw the Father doing in heaven, and Jesus is, after all, the only perfect image of the invisible God.

Here, in a nutshell, is the reality of all this. My experience of life as a praying Christian does not reveal the perfect image of the invisible God, only the Jesus of the Gospels can do that!

The church's sacraments and rituals do not reveal the invisible God. Our prayers, and our human wisdom and knowledge of root causes of illnesses do not reveal God to us. Our intimate working knowledge of the human body or useful secular counselling skills will not reveal God to us. Only the Jesus of the Scriptures will do this.

He healed everyone who asked him who had even a small degree of expectancy, without laying down any pre-conditions at all, and he claimed to be one with the Father. It is, therefore, always the Father's will to heal —always, and without exception or condition.

There is a battle within. I thought of the battle between his nature and his training that my guide dog had doubtless fought at the water's edge, and I thought of the inner battle those priests might well have fought on the banks of the promised land. And I reflect on the battle between experience and truth. Experience is the result of our everyday struggling lives as praying Christians, and truth is the content and expression of the New Testament. Experience and truth are not the same! Realising the difference is the start key to kingdom walking. This is the one step of obedience that God is calling for in all of us.

Like the priests of Joshua, we need to take one step. One single step away from our experience and towards the Gospel truth is enough to do it. Take that step, and all heaven breaks out around us. We begin to lay down the counterfeit image of the 'god' of our working knowledge and experience, the undependable one; and live in the kingdom life of the real, dependable Jesus whom we meet in the word of God. Take the first step, and the walls of evil, sickness and injury are ready to come tumbling down!

This was always my challenge: can I honestly approach sickness and injury, every single time, with the fullest assurance that God's answer is always 'Yes', and that nothing, absolutely nothing, can come between us and the love of God? Can I respond in prayer to a sick person, whatever they are suffering from, and know, in the depths of my stomach while I pray, that it is God's complete will to heal them? Do we realise absolutely that, as I begin to pray, a gift of healing is on the way from heaven?

This needs thinking about. This needs careful and honest consideration. This is not what I have learned, either from my experience of God or from the teaching of my elders and betters. This means picking up everything I ever knew about God and the church's healing ministry and being prepared to take a step forward into the unknown world of total trust. We have to be prepared to throw away everything but the revealed truth. One thing is for certain: the walker will know when he has taken the first step —the proof of the pudding is in the eating. Jericho's walls begin to tumble down with the most remarkable consistency!

It becomes paramount that I take this first step again and again every day of my life as a Christian. The promised land is crammed these days with 'Jerichos', or rather with ordinary innocent souls imprisoned within their apparently sky-high diseased and injured walls —and yet I will only pass this way once.

But in passing, I accrue a feeling of the enormous value of life, its possibilities and a share in God's great adventure —to turn the world back into the Eden state through the blessing of Calvary.

The vision of it seems to colour nearly every thought, many words and most of my deeds with a conviction of what is eventually to come. We must all search for that portion of divine grace which will make us a blessing to those who come after us, crowns for Christ that will secure for us the Lord's 'Well done, good and faithful servant' commendation in the adventure to come. But where to start?

Every single one of God's gently given revelations about the truth of his kingdom, and its reliable properties of healing, seem to be kept secret from us until they are released to us by our obedience. However hard I tried in the past, I simply failed to prise open these gifts by my training or my philosophy or my meditational thinking.

But as soon as any of us obey, as soon as we take those tiny first steps of faith into Jordan's dangerously swollen waters, a flash of light comes. Like the man in his speedboat, we can only let God's truth work in us by stepping into it and soaking in it, rather than by striving into it.

I have, over the years, read volumes on the work of the Holy Spirit and listened to endless lectures on the same subject when, as it turns out, what I really needed to put in was five minutes of drastic obedience. Then God begins to make things as clear as a sunbeam.

I have so often said to myself, 'I suppose I shall understand divine healing one day.' Now it begins. It is not study that makes the breakthrough into this kingdom living where the miraculous is commonplace, but obedience. The tiniest fragment of obedience, and heaven opens up, and the profoundest truths of God's kingdom are ours straight away. We are to take everything we think we know about healing ministry – the many things that we have been taught, and the conclusions we have come to based on past experiences – and step forward, prepared to lose for the sake of the 'promised land' whatever is not of God.

I called to my guide dog: 'Come on!' I took another step towards him in the quietly deepening water. 'Can I carry the harness?'

I slipped the buckle. He seemed to fly away from me in a shower of moonlit silver spray!

Chapter Five

THE FIRST STEP

In his wake I was left wet —and wondering about Joshua's priests. If only I could do what they did! One priestly foot in the water, one trembling, uncertain, fearful foot in the water, then would it part? And would thousands find their way past me to the promised land? Interestingly, they did not carry anyone across the river, they simply held up the true and living word of God.

That is what we are to do. It is not so much about counselling anyone or even praying for their healing, but about proclaiming the good news of Christ as our reliable Lord, Saviour and healer, in the face of rivers of doubt and unbelief. At this point I was thinking of the promised land not so much in terms of the everlasting life we shall enjoy in heaven, but, in this life, a kingdom promised by the saving, healing grace of Calvary, a land full of health and abundance of life. Would that not be every pastor's dream?

***

It had already been a long day by the time I stepped up onto the platform to give the keynote speech at the conference, but as is often the case, the speaker is quickly re-energised through the prayers of others, and away I went.

Somewhat to my surprise, a large crowd pressed forward for

healing prayer at the end of my talk, and those appointed to work with me were too small in number for this unexpected workload.

The timetable had slipped considerably by that point, as the worship had been deeply heartfelt and there had followed too many announcements. By eleven o'clock that night we were still working. Eventually my minder arrived on the stage alongside me and whispered authoritatively in my ear, "Mike, it's very late and you look grey. We are going back to the hotel. Now!" And we did.

The next lady in the queue had been rehearsing over and over what to say and was ready to speak. Seeing me leave the arena, she burst into tears. It now seems she had been waiting seven years for the moment when she knew in her heart that God would heal her, and her opportunity was disappearing in front of her eyes. Nearly an hour spent standing in the queue, and what seemed to her to be her one chance was going home! Seven years before, she had developed a thrombosis during childbirth and was left with phlebitis in one leg, swollen and painful, and encased in a surgical stocking all that time. In a humanly understandable flood of self pity and frustration she fled the conference arena to drive back to her hotel.

Meanwhile, I had been persuaded to sit a while in the foyer and unwind with a coffee and friends before going to my room, and this made the situation seem even worse. Unknown to me, that hurting lady and I were staying in the same hotel. She pushed through the swing doors into the foyer and my reclining, laughing form was the first thing she set eyes on. Inwardly, she confessed later, she exploded. 'Who is this arrogant man,' she thought, 'who walks away right at the moment I could have been healed, and now lies around laughing? He must have had the time for me; he is just wasting it now!' She marched off towards the elevator in tears, into her bedroom, threw herself on the bed in a flood of seemingly missed opportunity and woke up in the morning completely healed. Full of joy, she approached me at the start of the next day's business and told me this story of grace. I invited her to share it with all the conference delegates; she was far from daunted by the task and readily agreed to it. She finished her story by telling them, "One thing I've really learned through all this business last night," she turned towards me and grinned, "I've learned that this is absolutely nothing at all to do with you Mike, is it?" I clapped my hands for joy.

We had witnessed yet another case of 'shadow healing', the Holy Spirit graciously confirming the truth, without human intervention, of what I had been saying in the conference talk. Here is the truth of starting to go kingdom walking— if I lift up onto my shoulders everything I understand as being my image of a healing God, everything I have learned over years of ministry, and all that experience and knowledge that has compacted down into the depths of my being, and take one frightening, dreadful – and possibly intellectually humiliating – kingdom step of boldly proclaiming aloud the good news of Christ as our consistent and reliable Lord, Saviour and healer, then I should be opening the way for so many people to find the kingdom of promise, the land flowing with abundance, with Christ's health and restoration. The waters will part for them; they will come into a miraculous place that offers them healing.

Would everyone get healed? No, but a great deal more than there ever were before, and perhaps in potentially staggering numbers. What a dream! This ought to be realistically possible, because such a kingdom life flowed into ordinary people through ordinary people in New Testament days.

Kingdom restoration is a feature of the in-between times. When the second coming has happened there will be no healing because there will be no sickness. Our gracious Lord, through Calvary, provides us with a foretaste of that life by the ample and seemingly bottomless chest of healing graces. This will never be right for all of us but, when he comes back, we will not need this ministry any more anyway!

But how should we know what this single step of drastic obedience really is, that throws open the treasure trove? What was it for those early Christians? We want to make sure that we take the right step forward, the steady one, or everything we stand for might be swept away.

We know that Christ loves us and has freed us from our sins by his blood, and has made us to be a kingdom and priests to serve his God and Father, but one thing is for sure — that kingdom is a place of restoration because of Calvary, and we cannot afford to ignore that.

Let us revisit the scene, if we may, of that rich man dressed in fine clothes and living in luxury every day while the beggar lay at his gate, covered with sores and longing to eat the discarded scraps from the rich man's table. The street dogs come every day and lick his sores, so he is not only a poor beggar, he is sick, too.

When the beggar eventually dies, the angels carry him to Abraham's side in heaven. On the other hand, when the rich man died, he was in hell, where he was in agony. No amount of pleading his case could change the rich man's eternal situation. By then it was all too late for him. His fault? He must have walked in and out of his house every day, through his gates and straight past the poor and sick beggar. To him the sick must have become simply part of the landscape.

Heeding the awful warning in this story, no disciple of Christ can afford to allow the sick to become part of the landscape. Of course, compassion for those who suffer is not confined to the realms of Christianity by any means —to suggest such a thing would insult millions who love and care for friends and family alike. But the Christian has the message of the cross, and his life is lived in the open, not in a pious cubby-hole, and certainly not through whispered prayer in a hidden side chapel, tucked away from view!

Christ gave himself for us, saving us and empowering us, and we have to incarnate something of his sacrificially loving kingdom life. If we do not, then we have not really received him. That is the plain truth of it. The kingdom's whole drive and purpose is to draw the whole of creation back into the Eden state. That, after all, was the intent of the cross of Calvary, the beating heart of the kingdom of God. It was to make this possible, this place where there is no punishment, no poverty, no sickness, where there is everlasting life and the righteousness seen in Christ himself.

This is the promised land, the Eden state of things, the place across the river flowing in full spate. But we can get there. One right, obedient and fearful step of intense risk —and the waters part for thousands. Can we afford to take such a step? Can we deeply and seriously contemplate the thought of comparing everything we believe about healing grace – where it comes from and how it might affect people – little bit by little bit, and consider it in the light of Scripture?

This would be a journey not undertaken by many. For the sake of the sick and the injured, can we risk it? If we could shine a torch into the darkness ahead, then we might be encouraged rather than frightened by what we see. It is said that thousands of years ago, in the days of the Psalmists, night-time travellers wore oil lamps on the tops of their shoes, freeing themselves to hold their camel reins with one hand and their staff in the other. Each step ahead would reveal only where they were about to place their next footstep and very little more. But, when we are trying to stay safe in the darkness, it is enough. We may well be able to discern the general direction ahead by general star navigation, but that is not sharp enough to provide sufficient warning of potholes in the road. In our case, if true compassion encourages us to find effective answers for others, what will be our light? If we walk in the light of Jesus, we are in fellowship with him. In other words, those who walk in the kingdom will reflect his light. No one comes across the kingdom of God in the darkness but in the light.

Thankfully, the kingdom itself is not shrouded in mysterious darkness. God is light. He does not contain light, or prefer the light, or appreciate light. He is the light. Light has many characteristics: it is a particle; it is a wave; it illumines, burns, nourishes, heals, heats and reflects. We need it in these days to be an agent for revelation. The difficulty for us is that the dark has its own attractions, for all sorts of reasons.

Personally, I love it in the literal dark; it is a place where all things are equal. Nobody can see any better than I do in the dark. Nobody can find their way around a room and bump into fewer things than I do. I am the one who would not panic in a power cut! Strangely, I feel at an advantage in a darkened room because, over the years, I have developed the skills – the radar and spacial awareness – to navigate, a skill that others may not have. Nobody feels any safer than I do —we are all equal here. No one unintentionally puts me down or addresses me condescendingly because I am disabled, we are all in the same boat. In other words, this is a power thing; familiarity with the subject offers us security.

All those emotions can also be recognised in our theologies, especially those theologies concerning the supernatural. But can we afford to subject our ministry of healing to the light of Scripture? The threat of this sort of light is that it can seem so harsh, exposing all the imperfections in our deeds and in our beliefs. It can open up a whole can of worms! Privately we might handle that one —but in public? It seems much safer in the dark, where we can blend in and hide, where our shortfalls go unrecognised, most importantly by ourselves. It is easy to slide into the dark, where the sharp colours of our theology are subdued and the edges of our doctrine are blurred.

The less there is to know about us and how we think, the less there is to criticise. But light is really only an enemy to us when we imagine we have something to hide, or a position to lose. I sometimes wonder why the kingdom of God is such a shadowy concept for so many of us – a place to shy away from – when God describes himself as light. Perhaps we are in the dark about his kingdom because that is where we like to keep it. We may like the idea of being spiritual, knowing God somehow, and being in fellowship with him, but we may have little real, deep-down, urgent desire to be obedient to him.

Perhaps when we tell ourselves that miraculous things are mysterious it is our way of keeping him distant and cutting ourselves some theological slack. The less we know about God, the less we have to change. The less we accept the miraculous kingdom and its works today, the less we have to look vulnerable and weak and silly in front of other people. Unhappily, although we might like it in the dark, we know we cannot live there. Very little grows in the dark. Everything is dormant in the darkness that is spiritual winter.

We come into the world in a bright light, are brought up with nightlights and headlights and street lights and lighted road signs and torches and floodlights on our tallest buildings; all of them come to lance the black boil of night —and destruction of darkness is what the light of Jesus does. The true light is indeed Jesus himself, the word made flesh; it is also the Bible. The true light shows us the kingdom of God.

Our first step is one of being prepared to re-examine how we think about Jesus in the sharply focused light of the New Testament. This is not easy — we will have to set out on a long journey of fighting against every little extra piece of philosophical and theological deduction, checking it carefully against the Scriptures every inch of the way, until we eventually come back to the pure original. Surprisingly, when it comes to the healing ministry, most of us, in pew and pulpit alike, have drifted a very long way from the Gospel truth of miraculous things. It is not that we doubt God's power, it is just that we have very little expectancy that such things would ever happen. When at last we turn on the light, it takes a moment for our eyes to adjust. Things will look very different in the light, and we will be blinking and dazzled by the sight, because we see things as they actually are, and not as we imagined them. But what holds us back?

Remembering again the crossing of the river Jordan, the Reubenites, Gadites and the half tribe of Mannasseh held back. They had persuaded Moses to allow them to settle on the eastern bank. The fighting men had agreed to Joshua's condition of helping the main body of the Israelites but, after footholds in the promised land were secured, they were always going to return to the safer side. (See Joshua 1:12ff.) This was the side they knew. They had been here before. This was the land that suited their livestock. They would feel secure here. This was the place to be for them, the place of comfort they had reached after their wanderings. Moses had given them the land and it was safe. There was no need to change anything, they only had to pitch their tents, fortify the local towns against any threat, and all would be well.

Many of us have grown into an analogous situation of ease over what we know about miraculous healing. We understand what we understand, and the last thing we need is for it to be challenged. We have worked out our own theologies, they fit our everyday circumstances and we like them. We think we know, wrongly as it turns out, that God does not always want to heal the sick; we 'know' that many of our prayers seem to us to meet with heavenly silence. The more cynical, intellectual and educated speak up: 'You don't really believe in all this miraculous stuff, do you?' It has become a smart thing to spend the energy of one's argument in sceptical questioning instead of humble searching. But it is only the intellectually childlike and the spiritually impoverished who will see the value of the land across the river.

The intellectual cynic will find his place with the Reubenites' wives and cattle. We have a God we claim is good. We claim that he is love, and that he is no preferer of persons. And yet some are visibly divinely blessed, whilst some, outwardly, may not appear to us to be. So, in an attempt to overcome these sorts of 'contradictions', we tend, unwisely, to do God's thinking for him. We suppose that he must have other plans for certain sick people than simply healing them, or that it is a matter of his timing.

The trouble is that none of these suppositions exist in Jesus' ministry. They only serve to make a tangled mess, full of doubt, confusing us and tripping us up —doubt being that most powerfully damaging single blockage!

Again, we may believe that sickness is a prerequisite of our dying, or that sickness comes from God as a discipline, or is a gift for strengthening us. All these giant thoughts are strongholds against our crossing the river. They hold us back. They mean that we have the wrong image of God to whom we pray.

We have wandered round in the wilderness for so long that we find it hard to believe that there could ever be such a place as Canaan, the promised land, the Eden state of affairs; some even begin to doubt the reliability and consistency of God. There is little evidence of trust and hope that the kingdom is a more fruitful place than the wilderness we are used to living in. Some of us have even poked our noses over the border and come running home in fear, telling all who will listen to us that the world of the miraculous is full of strange and disfigured souls. But then such pastors have to bear the responsibility of driving the people out again into the wilderness for another forty years. Many of them will probably die without ever seeing this kingdom on earth, real though it surely is. Could God ever say this to us? —"Woe to you, teachers of the law and Pharisees, you hypocrites! You shut the kingdom of heaven in men's faces. You yourselves do not enter, nor will you let those enter who are trying to. Woe to you, teachers of the law and Pharisees, you hypocrites! You travel over land and sea to win a single convert, and when he becomes one, you make him twice as much a son of hell as you are" (Matthew 23:13-15).

None of this should be at all surprising. Most of us have built in our minds an image of God and his kingdom out of our experiences of being Christians. From this we draw the erroneous conclusion that the answers to our prayers are unreliable and inconsistent and so that is how God is. We could hardly be more mistaken, but this way of thinking, sadly, has a momentum of its own. If we pray to a wrong 'image' of God rather than the true and living God, nothing happens, and that wrong image is seemingly confirmed and strengthened by our experience. As a direct consequence, even less happens in answer to prayer, and around we go again.

For some people, praying for sick and injured friends and relatives seems like a matter of chance. Faced with no change, then, the thought comes that it was worth a go!

Of course such thoughts as these may be unrecognised, unformulated and unspoken in the hearts of the modern Christian, in case they prove disrespectful of God or of the individual's faith, so we wrap up the uncomfortable parcel in the attractive paper of philosophical second-guessing about the alternative purposes of God. We cannot see that every one of these thoughts is a stronghold, a thick rope that ties us back into where we are —failing to believe in the fruitfulness of what might be ours, and unwilling to take a step and cross over. And here is the problem. Our *experience* of being Christians may not in itself be sufficient to ensure that we have an accurate knowledge of the invisible God, the Father of our Lord Jesus Christ. Experience needs to be evaluated in the light of the word.

We have built many of our practical working beliefs on our experiences, and tend to proclaim that the promised land cannot be fruitful, as we have been wandering around it for many years and know what it is like!

To make the situation even worse, we may have been teaching people that they should not have too high an expectancy of the kingdom in case there is disappointment! But, if we have never crossed over, we may well believe that the other side of the river must be the same as this one.

However, there is only one reliable image of God, his will and his strength, and that is the character of Jesus himself as described to us in the Gospels.

All our experiences of the Christian life, all we understand about the kingdom of God today, must be submitted to what is revealed in the word, in Jesus. Our 'need' to hold onto the wrong image – to maintain ungodly beliefs we might have held for years – has to be dealt with. We have to take our courage in both hands as this can be a scary process.

Consider the commonly held belief that the unhealed are actually being subjected to some other mystical heavenly plan, or that God is somehow blocked by their sin, or their 'need' for punishment. But what did Jesus do? If we are prepared to let go of all our intellectual and spiritual calculations, our excuses and philosophies, we can see at once that Jesus never refused to heal anyone who asked him for that grace. Some people may have had doubts, but he never refused to help them out of their situations. He healed them all, unconditionally. Do we begin to sense a struggle inside us between the two images of God? Which one is the stronger? Are we trying to find a satisfying counter argument?

Here is a well tried one— no fewer than three times in Matthew's Gospel the word 'many' is used to describe how many were healed. 'Wonderful!' we sigh with relief, 'Many is not all, so he did not heal everyone!' But, 'Be still, fighting heart!' No, Jesus did not heal everyone, he healed everyone who asked with some little degree of expectancy. That is different. How many in the crowd, like us, had too much doubt, too much unbelief? As in Nazareth, how many could not be reached? The spirit of the message remains: God's will is to heal all who come in expectancy to Jesus.

If we go on believing that we have a God who picks and chooses who he blesses, then we will never be able to come to him with childlike expectancy, and consequently we will never see the kingdom in the fullness of its working glory. This is quite contrary to the commonly held idea that God does not wish to heal everybody. Jesus healed all who came to him seeking healing. He did and said what he saw the Father doing, and he rebuked his disciples who had not recognised that when they looked at him they were seeing the perfect image of the Father in heaven. The only sensible and logical deduction we can make from the words and works of Jesus is that God wishes to see healed all who come to Jesus for healing. The image of God we tend to cling onto is far more complicated and unreliable than the truth! So when we pray for healing we must believe in the absolute reliability and consistency of Jesus —and not doubt, because when we doubt we are like a wave on the sea, blown and tossed about by the wind.

We may be in two minds here: on the one hand we proclaim a scriptural Jesus, who reliably works wonders, and on the other we worship one we think might or might not do so. In this frame of double-mindedness we cannot expect to receive anything from him.

Another common misunderstanding is that God requires us to become 'better' people before healing us. We might think we are too insignificant, too lowly, too unforgiving, or that there is some sin in our past which is not yet repented of. This is our mistaken idea of God which arises from our 'making excuses' for his apparent failure to offer healing.

In ministry today we tend to take a long and often fruitless route. We begin to search for the sin behind the sickness. We meet someone with a stiff neck and we conclude Old Testament disobedience when they might actually have been sleeping in a draught! We come across aching shoulders and explain to the sufferer that they have not yet laid down some burden before the Lord. More likely they have done too much heavy gardening! Bad knees, we discern, may well be the result of kneeling to false gods, when they might be a sports injury. Similarly we find arthritic conditions and tell the supplicant to go and search out areas of unforgiveness in their lives, and so on. The blind become blind because they are frightened of seeing something and the deaf cannot hear for fear of some bad news or other —and so it goes on and on within the realms of the modern so-called healing ministry. None of this clever – and apparently spiritual – 'discernment', however, can be found in Jesus' ministry. It would be absurd to suppose that the modern church knows better and has become more 'spiritual' in these things! Our true heavenly Father, perfectly revealed by Jesus in the Gospel accounts, never asked anyone to straighten their lives out first. Divine love and grace are too great for that. But because Christ, the true image of God, is so trustworthy and faithful, the church's message to the sick and injured cannot be hit and miss, 'yes and no'. The Son of God, Jesus Christ, was not 'yes and no' —in him it has always been 'Yes.'

No matter how many promises God has made, they are 'Yes' in Christ. So this is the first step into effective kingdom walking: we begin by simply and humbly recognizing that any unbiblical image of God we may have adopted – as one to whom praying is often hard and often fruitless work – is not the true God. We may have done our business with him for many a long year, and for you he may seem to be all there is. But we must pick up all our understandings of him and turn back to the Gospel. We have to learn to take each tiny concept we have adopted of how he and his ministry work, and compare it to him. We must be prepared to abandon any long-held belief that does not exactly fit the life pattern of the Jesus we find in Scripture —the perfect image of the invisible God. Only then will the waters begin to part.

It is desperately vital that we step into the water; thousands are standing on the river bank waiting for us. And the danger?

Chapter Six

EYESIGHT CHECK-UP

The kingdom of God, this cross-centred and consequently abundant spiritual acreage of restoration, is the most fascinating place in which to spend one's days. It is exciting, enthralling, possessive, magnetic, thrilling and joyful, full of incident and overflowing with glory to the Son of God. It is a miraculous place, literally; it is heaven on earth and every Christian is invited to live there.

The great danger facing all of us who do not long to take this kingdom step, but who long to stay with the Reubenites on the eastern shore, is not that we shall make a complete failure of life, nor that we shall fall back into out-and-out secularism, nor be terribly unhappy —none of these things. The real danger is that we may miss grasping life's greatest meaning, be unable to reach its highest good, miss out on its deepest and most lasting joy; so we would not be equipped to serve, we would be unaware of life on fire with the light of the presence of the kingdom of God, and be content to have it like this —that is the danger.

It is frightening to think that one day we could wake up and find that we have been so busy with the trappings and husks of church life that we have missed life itself.

Life without our vibrant, active and restoring God, for anyone who has known the joy and richness of walking with him in his miraculous Eden-style kingdom on earth, would be impossible and unthinkable. That sort of life is what I pray my fellow Christians may be spared —satisfaction with a life that falls somewhere short of the best.

***

With a sigh, Maggie flopped down in the armchair and told me, "I'm eighty six now, and my dear husband is ninety, so I suppose a few things are just bound to go wrong! Anyway, let me tell you. My right eye has a huge black disc in the middle of it that I can only just see around the outside, and the left eye has two of them, side by side. I can just see a bit of light around the outside of these discs. That's all that's left to me."

"I'm so sorry, I said, "This must be a terrible shock for you?"

She grinned at me. "Yeah," she sighed, "I suppose I'll have to give up driving the truck soon!"

So we began to pray. I did not really know if I trusted Jesus enough to do this, but we gave it a go anyway.

In Psalm 50 we are told to 'Sacrifice thank-offerings to God'; and he says, '...call upon me in the day of trouble; I will deliver you, and you will honour me.' So we began to praise the Father for Jesus, and gave thanks for what our Saviour and healer achieved on Calvary. In a short while I plucked up enough courage to ask her, "Maggie, what's happening?" She told me that the disc in the right eye was getting smaller. I kept a straight face and a suitably sombre tone but I really wanted to jump up and run around the room, screaming with teenage delight!

"Then let's go on," I encouraged her. Five minutes more of praise and thanksgiving went by and she could see perfectly through the right eye. Thrilled to my socks I asked her, "Maggie, the two discs on the left, which one would you like the Lord to do first?" This was not an attempt on my part to manipulate God, it was an outburst of excited trust.

"The right one, please!" Away we went again with praise and thanksgiving, quietly and gently, as might befit a ministry to a lady of a certain age and delicacy.

"How are we doing, Maggie?" I asked her after a little while.

"Oh, fine," she told me, "it's almost gone."

Then we started on the last remaining disc. This one was a bit sticky and took a while to budge, but in the end it did. Perfect vision returned to both eyes. I called her husband into the room.

Taking one look and seeing very quickly what had happened, he knelt at Maggie's feet, took her hands in his, rested his head in her lap and they sobbed together with joy until there were no more tears to be had from either of them.

'But where is this kingdom?' you may ask. 'I want it too!' you may shout. 'How can I live like that?' you may wonder. 'Does such a restoring place really exist on this decaying planet or in what might seem to many at first glance to be a decaying church organisation?' Is the answer to go out and buy a book on the subject? You may be wondering: If it really does exist in any form other than religious theory in books, where is the evidence of that? What can I see? What truth can I hear? Is all this talk of the kingdom merely clerical philosophising? Where are the signs of it and where do I go to stand and wonder at it? Is the kingdom on earth a state that just sounds romantic and wonderful? It sounds rather like an unassailable plateau rising vertically out of an impenetrable jungle, promising all sorts of adventures. Is it a sort of 'lost world'? To most people I think it might be!

Surely, if we look around us, we ought to see the evidence: many stories like Maggie's. If it really is true, and not merely the theory of preachers and publications, then it will leave traces behind it in the world. Christ gave so much to bring it here and leave it here: there must be signs of his kingdom visible here on earth. The kingdom must indeed be around here somewhere and we will not find it in man's books but in simple, trusting and compassionate hearts.

A Christian has to choose between three options at this point. We can learn all about the theory of the kingdom, or we can set out to find it, or we can ignore the whole thing. I was always a bear with a small brain and as inquisitive as a cat, so I find it the greatest fun to go out and look.

Now, if I wanted to travel to see one of the famous wonders of the world I would expect to discover two things on the way there. I would hope to find signposts to direct me and I would expect to marvel at what I saw when I arrived. If there were not signs at regular intervals I would soon get lost on the journey, and if there were no wonder on my arrival I would ask myself what all the fuss was about.

Some of the signs and wonders of the kingdom seem to go unnoticed. Or do they? My mind races back to the end of a long day's teaching at a cathedral in north Wales. We were packing up to go home, the ministry had finished, the books sold and the tapes ordered, and all that remained was to thank our hosts and go home.

Visitors often mill about at the back of cathedrals, sightseeing on a spare afternoon and buying the odd postcard. As I was walking somewhat wearily back down the centre aisle of the cathedral, one such lady, passing by, accosted me, saying, "I don't know what you are doing, I don't belong to your faith, but it looks like some sort of healing thing. Can you heal me?" she asked.

"What's wrong?" I enquired.

She had cancer of the throat. She told us that each time she swallowed it was like swallowing a golf ball. Incurable, inoperable and painful, she added.

I took her hands and with others began to glorify Jesus for all that he had shown us and done for us. She watched us, somewhat bemused. After a while I asked her, "How does that feel?"

She swallowed, and reported, "Just the same."

Six times I prayed. Six times I asked her and six times she swallowed and reported no change. Still holding her hands I turned my head to ask a friend to do some praying. I was thinking, 'How do I close this down? This is really not going to happen! How do I extricate myself from this situation gracefully? How do I leave her in some sort of positive state of hope?'

Before I could say anything she blurted out, "Thank you!"

"What for?" I thought she was just being polite to me.

"Just as you turned your head just now it seemed to come loose. I swallow and it isn't there any more!"

"Thanks be to Jesus," I got his name in again quickly but she was turning to leave.

I wonder if she ever saw the sign to the kingdom? I wonder if she ever came back to Jesus in wonder and thanks?

So, to me, the navigational challenges of going off to live in the kingdom on earth will be easy —I will have signs to point out the way and wonders to confirm that I have found the right thing. But why is this journey such a lonely one? Where are all the others? Where is the crowd that flocks to find the kingdom, that they can be sustained in it? The thing about 'signs', of course, is that we are supposed to see them, and this brings up a most important point. Anyone setting out to see something must be able to see! I do not know that anyone will be entirely convinced if they cannot follow the signs, and marvel in wonder when they arrive! We must get ourselves fit for the journey – we must have our eyes checked out, or we will at best not appreciate the glories we see, or at worst will get lost on the way.

So let us begin by thinking about sight. Remember that we are spirit, soul and body. The first thing we must take to heart before we will ever properly appreciate the kingdom is that we can only hold the kingdom in true focus with the eyes of the spirit. This is critical. We are used to looking around us with the eyes of body and soul. We are carnal: we tend to evaluate with our physical eyes and with the eyes of the understanding of the mind or soul, with which we make judgements about what we see, touch, hear, feel or smell. But we will never properly see the kingdom using any or all of our five senses, together with the judgement of human wisdom, experience and learning. It is constantly attempted but it simply cannot be done. There are many things in this world of which we are unaware, such as certain high frequency noises which cannot be picked up by the human ear —so we sometimes think we are in a place of silence when it is not necessarily so. We would need other sensitive devices to pick up those sounds. The kingdom of God is not even of this world, and we would be foolish, therefore, to imagine that we can discern it carnally, through our senses and our learning. It is the eye of the spirit that will see it.

So how do we see with our spiritual eyes? By focusing them on the word of God. There is simply no other way. Simply reading it is insufficient, as is measuring it against our experiences. We must work hard at throwing away our negative prayer experiences, and work equally hard at accepting and believing the message in all its simplicity. Having thus re-focused our spiritual senses on the word of God, we must take the greatest care not to allow the mistiness of the old carnal understandings to wash the words away. Their truth must remain with us in childlike simplicity and clarity. If it does not, then that childlike, joyful acceptance will turn into intellectual exercise again, and sight of the kingdom will be lost.

Consider how this loss may occur. The Gospels show clearly that Jesus was willing and able to heal everyone who came to him asking for that grace. We also know that he taught faith (expectancy) to be a major function in healing the sick, and had trouble doing healing ministry in the face of unbelief. That all seems very simple until our minds attempt to use that picture to account for our observation that some people today do not seem to be able to get healed. It is at this point that we cease to be spiritual and revert to being carnal. Then, with a sense of relief, we might fall upon the verses in Matthew's Gospel that report his healing 'many who were there'. We might then conclude that the word 'many' is not the same as the word 'all' and that therefore Jesus did not heal everyone who asked. We leave the argument as a happier soul, carnally satisfied, ignoring the fact that 'many' means a large number, and blinded to the possibility that the others were not healed because they may have been too unbelieving. Then again, they might not have asked.

The tendency to rationalise like this, the inclination to make judgements about God's ways according to our experiences as Christians – and not with a simple, childlike understanding of Scripture – can easily prevent us from seeing the kingdom in its fullness and keep us from ministering out of its wealth into the lives of those around us who crave it. If we know what we understand, and then try to make the Scriptures (and our theology) fit our existing carnal understanding, we find that such arrogance will blind the spiritual eye.

So let us suppose, first of all, that we have reached a place where we can see that the kingdom, as displayed in Christ, is a reliable and wondrous restoring place of consistent miracles and truth. Suppose, too, we are prepared to lay down in humility the fact that we think life simply is not like that today; and then accept for a moment that it may have been we who have changed and not God. Now we are in a position to take a tentative step towards life in the kingdom.

This is not easy. We all have experience of prayer. We all know that much of our prayer does not seem to get through the roof, let alone as far as the clouds. We all know that prayer for others, at least outside the family, is all too often an act of Christian duty; it can be hard work that carries its own levels of guilt when we slip in our faithfulness and carry silent shame over our ineffectiveness. We keep quiet about these feelings, but we have no idea why we feel like that.

But then it gets much worse. Instead of keeping our spiritual eye on Jesus as we see him in the Gospels – on his reliability and great power to work miracles, and on his unchanging nature – we begin to make 'excuses' for God, for seemingly unanswered prayer. We work out with our carnal minds and emotions that he has other ideas these days than immediate restoration, and we think that his view of sickness must have changed. When this approach does not appear entirely appropriate, we turn our blaming toward the supplicant. Notwithstanding the teaching of the New Testament, we start claiming that there must be blockages that come between them and the love of God. In all this we build a false picture of God as being powerless to help. Thus we teach of him, we discuss him, we pray to him —and in so doing we fail the flock. We teach them to use their carnal attributes to measure God —so they fail, too.

In general, the extensive failure in the Church's so-called healing ministry and miracle working is that, as a consequence of its carnality, it sets out to find the way from man to God. Starting with man in his condition, it tries to find a way up to the holiness of heaven, discerning and overcoming assumed obstacles on the journey; but there is no through road to be discovered that way. In the end we are left with a 'ministry' the end of which is ineffectual, rather than the shining joy of healing.

Nowhere can we see the difference in vision more obviously than when we watch Christians while they themselves are watching other Christians working miracles. Those with spiritual sight are overcome with joy and amazement, and they give thanks and glory to God; those who see carnally are disliking the style of ministry or sensing criticism of the worship or the type of prayer being used. They even cast doubt on the word being preached while the Holy Spirit is still in the business of confirming it himself with signs and wonders in front of them! Those who see spiritually go out with joy, while those who see carnally go out in doubt, disbelief and judgement.

Having discovered the right way to see, we have to turn that ability into movement. Otherwise we become people who listen to the word and do not do what it says. This would be like looking at ourselves in a mirror, going away and immediately forgetting what we look like. But if we can look intently into the perfect law that gives freedom – and keep on doing this, not forgetting what we have seen and learnt, but doing it – we will be blessed in what we do.

So, having geared ourselves to look intently into the perfect law of love which gives freedom, we have to take a step of faith and do what we have been told to do. In the moment when we take that step, the waters will part in front of us and we can step over on dry ground into the promised land. Joshua proved this on his way to sack Jericho. Elijah and Elisha did it on that very same river, smacking the surface of the water with a rolled-up cloak. Peter and the others proved it when stepping out of the boat and when feeding the five thousand. Our steps extend the kingdom and our expectancy is vital.

But we must be prepared to follow the biblical example here. Look at the way Joshua laid out his forces and then encouraged them onwards into a humanly impossible situation! He established the worship in front, followed by the priests who were carrying the ark (the word of God). As soon as the first priest put his foot cautiously into the Jordan, which was running at full spate, the waters backed up away from them —and the whole army crossed over.

As we begin to walk in the kingdom, we have to understand how to do it. We may have been used to singing songs and hymns, reciting liturgy and performing ecclesiastical ceremonies in church. We may have been doing good, carrying Christ into the community and helping the poor, but that is how we walk out our faith, not how we walk into the kingdom. What's the difference? When we walk in the kingdom there are two things we notice: the miraculous and glory. We see ordinary people restored, and they give glory to Christ.

We must be careful not to succumb to yet another tempting thought, or we will fool ourselves we are walking in the kingdom when it is not so: a temptation is to water down both essential components— the miraculous and the glory. We reduce the meaning of 'restoration' by just claiming a greater 'peace' as a result of our listening, when God's will is to restore us to the original blueprint state which obtained in the garden of Eden. We are too easily satisfied that we are giving the glory to God, when in reality the supplicant, the one who receives, needs to glorify him too.

Walking in the kingdom is always a matter of thanksgiving and praise, a complete focus on the message of the cross, and the courage to step into humanly impossible situations. The result is not merely 'nice' but miraculous, and the glory flows Godward by the bucketful!

Chapter Seven

PRESSING HOME

Beth stood a little tentatively in front of me, half wondering what was going to happen next. Some of the congregation slid to the edge of their seats in expectation while others slumped forward, elbows on knees, in an attitude of prayer. I reached out and took her hands lightly in mine and asked her, "What can we pray for?"

Beth, it turned out, is a potter; not just an ordinary hobby potter or even a skilled artist potter; she is a Christian potter, living on faith, who plies her business in churches all over the world, encouraging the faithful with the help of her potter's wheel and a great deal of clay, her powerful visual aid.

"Thing is," she whispered so that not everyone in the congregation could hear her, "my work is so public and everyone can see me doing it." That set me wondering. Of course I could not see whatever it was that she was referring to; I could only wait hopefully for further enlightenment.

"Look," she added eventually, "look at the tumour on my finger." I moved the ball of my thumb as gently and as lightly as I could along the outside of her index finger and there it was, between the first and second knuckle, a larger lump about the size of a very acceptable brussels sprout. She winced as my thumb passed over it.

"What does it look like?" I turned to the lady working with me. "Is it bad?" Apparently it was a bright, ruddy mauve; the skin had stretched so tightly over the growing tumour that the covering skin had turned transparent in its thinness.

Beth began again, "This is the second one on that spot. I had one before and in the end I had it surgically removed. The operation left a nasty scar but you can't see that now the new tumour has come."

Referring to the immediate possibility of prayer, she added, "The best I can hope for is that God will stop it growing any bigger!"

Well, I was not going to accept that remark any more than I believe Jesus might want to accept the tumour. We can find, in the writings of the ancient prophets, the idea that God enters into the sufferings of his people. The New Testament goes further and tells us that God is love. But that is not a love which, in the presence of suffering, can stand aloof from it. Past experience of prayer may lead us to believe that he is simply an observer, but the doctrine that Christ is the image of the invisible God means that God is compassionately engaged with us. Our wounds become his wounds, and in his death they die, too.

"Beth!" I exclaimed to her, remembering just in time to keep my voice down as, for all I know, she might well have been embarrassed if everyone watching was able to hear the conversation. "When did Jesus ever tell a leper that the best he could do would be to stop the leprosy getting any worse? And where in Scripture does Jesus say that he can only do his best and hope that it would be good enough?"

Beth grinned and giggled in a slightly shame-faced sort of way and the prayer began. Well, I use the word 'prayer' but the way we like to do it, the way we like to see the kingdom of God coming near, would not be called 'prayer' in the normal way of things. Kingdom work is a lot less like asking for healing and a lot more like thanksgiving. Kingdom children are not the sort to keep asking for a bicycle for Christmas when the father of the household announced years ago that he's built a cycle factory next door and we can have any sort of bike we need on free issue!

"Thank you, Father, for Jesus.... Thank you that he has taken all our pain and carried all our diseases and, because of his wounds, we are healed."

Do I mean to imply here that I have found a more effective 'formula'? Do I mean to manipulate God? That question is best answered with another to the reader: have you ever tried manipulating God? Am I encouraging the style of 'name it and claim it'? No, I am not thanking him for the healing of any particular wound of which we cannot see the evidence as yet. I take the last verse of Psalm 50, to which we referred earlier, to be a clear instruction to pray like this. It says,

> He who sacrifices thank-offerings honours me,
> and he prepares the way
> so that I may show him the salvation of God.

Thanksgiving makes way for the Lord. And to me the salvation of God is the sum of everything our Lord won for us on the cross, and that includes healing. He has taken all our pain and carried all our diseases and by his wounds we are healed.

There have been a number of church leaders and theologians who love to argue the point: was all the freedom for physical healing given at Calvary? But the writings of Matthew and Peter, two men who walked with Jesus, convince me that Jesus did indeed achieve this end. All I did with Beth was sacrifice thank offerings, but I did it with the full knowledge that the work of Calvary is complete. I trusted, therefore, that she would be healed.

At this point I would ask the reader to keep a wide view of the theology of all this— Jesus' teaching reminds us that only those of us who can approach the kingdom of God with childlike simplicity are ever going to get a handle on it! To leap at this point into thoughtful and intelligent discussion about types of prayer and traditional church ways of thinking about these things is usually disastrous for the supplicant. The kingdom seems to retreat from the sight of the straining of the human brain!

Now that I had gone on with the thanksgiving prayer for a little while, I felt a prompting to ask, "How are we doing?"

Beth hesitated; she did not quite know how to answer this. She, not unlike most of the flock who might accept prayer for healing, had never before heard a minister actually expect there to be any immediate change for the better!

My number two, the lady working with me, jumped into the conversation and suggested that Beth have a look and take stock. She opened her eyes and squeaked, "I think it's a bit smaller!"

"Shall we go on?" I asked her, teasingly. Such a question is always worth asking as we Europeans can get terribly embarrassed by too much attention being paid to us in public and, in a short while, everything inside us begins to scream loudly at us to go back into the congregation and sit down where we are not the centre of attention or holding up the queue any more!

"Yes, please!" came the now serious reply. So on we went. No requests, no begging, no searching for discernment of God's will, no naming and no claiming, just thanksgiving in trust. The proclamation of the good news of Christ even became embedded in our thanksgiving:

"Thank you Jesus that, in the moment of your dying, the curtain in the temple was torn in two from top to bottom. Not only did this allow access by us to you but it enabled the river of healing grace to flow out from under the throne of grace, down the middle of the street in heaven, underneath the tree with the leaves for the healing of the nations, back through that torn curtain into this world and into this church and all over Beth.... Now, Beth, tell me what that's like?"

It is worth pointing out that the words we use in prayer do not do it for us; the style does not do it for us; the childlike acceptance in trust meets the outpouring of grace from heaven, and that is what 'does' it.

Beth was excited now. The mauve colour had all gone, the skin was tight again. "Look!" she almost cried, "I can just see the scar from the previous operation but it's a lot smaller than it ever was before!" Two minutes more and it was completely restored.

The congregation was so thrilled they clapped; they applauded the risen King; they expressed their delight in the only way they could at that moment. And these were not uncontrollable teenagers, they were middle-aged and older than that, people whom one might think would naturally be able to control themselves in public! I felt that I needed to explain something to them.

"Now sometimes people do not appreciate my style of doing

things – I mean all this praying in public and out loud, right in front of everyone. At the very least, in the denomination I was brought up in. You should have expected me to come here today in my robes and take these dear ones off quietly into the Lady Chapel. So I want you to know how I feel about that. Signs and wonders of the kingdom were not invented by God to be hidden amongst a quiet group of robed officials in a side chapel. If they are kept quiet they're pointless. What good is a sign or a wonder if no one sees it? If you're driving down a highway trying to find London and I hide the signpost behind a tree, would you thank me for that? Jesus tells us to set our lamp on a table and not hide it so that men may see our good works and give glory to our Father who is in heaven. The Holy Spirit is bringing healing here so that we will give glory to Jesus. Is that OK?"

My number two said quietly, "There's another lady coming up to see us."

I held out my hands and Jean put her tiny ones back into mine. "How can we help?" I asked her.

"Two things, please. I have a twisted spine and there is so much arthritis in my knees that I can't bend them."

"How much can you do without it hurting? Can you show us? It's just that then we have something to test after we've done the business. Now, don't do more than is easy for you – we don't want you hurting yourself."

She tried to stoop and bend her knees just a little but gasped with the pain. A few paces behind me was the table, three steps up, and I asked her to climb to it. My helper stood, holding her hand to steady her, but she could not even lift her right foot onto the first low step without wincing with the pain.

Right through my whole body I could hear the cry of the two blind men following Jesus, calling out to him, "Have mercy on us, Son of David!"

Back she came. The thanksgiving sacrifice began again, along the same lines as it had been with Beth a few minutes earlier. In a little while my helper took her hand and, very slowly and very gingerly, they climbed the steps to the altar table together.

Realising that something might actually happen here if she went on with this a bit longer, Jean asked for more of the holy kingdom treatment.

Now this is important. Jesus longs for us to be persistent about these kingdom things and yet temptation tries to put an end to it all as quickly as possible. Temptations sing in any minister's ear: 'Be thankful for what you've got and pack it in! Tell her the rest is probably on the way and get her to go and sit down! Pray for her to be filled with the Holy Spirit —maybe she'll fall over backwards and you can move along to the next one! Here's another idea: why not tell her that this will be slow but it's all in God's timing. Tell her that God is in control and that he knows what he is doing.'

The trouble is that this is all untrue. It is widely taught, much accepted and well used nonsense. This is not Jesus, and it does not reflect the good news of the message of the cross. In fact Jesus uses two separate parables to teach that persistence is a necessary part of prayer, and even demonstrates it with the blind man who saw men who looked like trees. Our Lord and healer got half way with him, checked the progress and then went on to complete the work.

So why should we be persistent? Because we need to press home. Every Christian knows full well that there is a distance between heaven and earth; there is a gap that requires application of the Spirit to cross. Remember that the prodigal son was living in a foreign country and had a way to travel before he met his father.

As well as all that, we need to understand the kingdom dynamic here. As we apply ourselves to pressing into heaven, our heavenly Father finds our insistence to be irresistible, and presses back the other way. It is exactly the same kingdom dynamic that we see in the parable of the prodigal son: the son moves towards home with a new intent and the father responds. As we push on into the gap between heaven and earth, so God pushes back towards us to find us somewhere in the middle of all this.

In another meeting I asked a man to come and stand with me while I demonstrated the principle of half way meeting and coming together like this —with a bath sponge. As I pressed into it with my fingertips, so he could not help but press back with his the other way. It is a normal reaction. As we pressed persistently towards each other the sponge became thinner and thinner until, as we worked at it, we could almost feel each other's fingertips. At the moment we touched, the symbolism of all this struck him, giving him a sense of its significance. It dawned on him, deep in his soul, that healing is nothing to do with our trying to get to God —it is all about letting him get to us. In that very moment, according to x-rays taken that very evening, two tumours in his lungs disappeared completely.

This 'renewal' business of quick pray and drop, this sacramental business of anoint and go, this charismatic foraging around in prayer for the reason for God's delay and seeming reluctance —none of this is from Scripture. It short-circuits the intent and dynamic of heaven and none of it is of the kingdom. Faith and trust say to us, 'Press on!'

The second time Jean tried the steps she managed them tentatively but unaided. On her coming back down from the raised table, someone in the congregation shouted out, "Her back is straight!"

On the third attempt, after yet more thanksgiving prayer to give glory to Jesus for what he has done for us on the cross, she ran up the steps, placed her hands on the table, said "Thank you!" —and skipped back down again.

I wanted so much to encourage the congregation. It is so easy to look at the speaker and believe that they must be especially anointed —it is a wonderful escape mechanism from our responsibilities, to claim that one person can do kingdom miracle working but not another.

We are in real danger of forgetting the cross. We love to admire the person on the platform but there is no power there of any value. The power is in the message of the cross. We will always remember it as a fact of history, it took place right enough, and is remembered in the sacrament of Holy Communion —but its message? The glorious message is that, once and for all, the curtain is torn. The river flows. God's hand is off the tap now. It does not matter one jot who I am or where I have been, what I have done or what I have been through —the river flows back through that curtain and all over me, and over the reader of this book, and over everyone in the congregation of the Lord. There is nothing, absolutely nothing, that can come between us and the love of God.

"Listen!" I said to them as they began to show signs of wanting to drift out of the sanctuary on their way to the interval coffee pots in the foyer. "The presence of Jesus in me is exactly the same as in you. By definition, Christians have within us the Spirit of Christ, and he develops in us the mind of Christ. And there's one thing we can easily tell about the mind of Christ from the Gospels: it has a great compassion for the sick. The anointing is not on me, it's on the whole church! Enjoy your coffee!"

As they went, the thought crossed my mind: how can I be so bold with the kingdom and yet remain in a proper place of humility? How is it that the words humble and bold can be used in the same sentence to describe someone? How can we be both these things at one and the same time? The answer, I believe, is because of the need of the hour and the quality of the workman. God finds the way to a human heart to lie through the heart of another. And therefore the need can only be fulfilled through us. That thought alone must surely be sufficient to induce humility.

It is not that we must be naturally bold characters, but rather that the act of preaching itself must be the bold sharing of the good news of the message of the cross. If it does not break through the defensive shields of the 'kingdom not-so-sures' it is of no value. It will be mere rhetoric. So I will go on being more than happy to wear sackcloth and ashes even as I swing my axe into the gates of hell.

Chapter Eight

THE PRIESTLY ROLE
IN HEALING

How is it that *some* people can stand in front of a physical disease, armed only with the power of the glorious message of the cross, and the illness begins to fade away in front of them? How I have longed to be in a position like that, a place where I, in tandem with Christ, can banish other people's pain! But the mind gets so mixed up with a thousand tumbling thoughts around this subject, a whirlpool of confusion brought about through one thing alone: our almost complete lack of experience over many centuries, although we are Christians, in the field of the supernaturally miraculous. We see it occasionally, and so, by definition, we discuss it at length from a place of ignorance of its practice; we are so afraid of it, we do not trust it, we suspect everything. We argue against it in order that we might not go over but stay on the eastern river bank with the Reubenite cattle, safe from any personal or spiritual perils ahead, real or imagined.

Nevertheless, while it is often easy for us to criticise the rest of the institutional church, if we do not sometimes despair of it, we should never forget that many graces, possibilities and powers really do exist within its walls, often chained up, lying dormant like frozen assets or tied-up capital. Performing miracles, to use the biblical expression, is only one of them.

Nevertheless, the private thought remains: would it not be lovely to be in a position with Christ to banish, sickness and injury from those who ask us for prayer? Most of us would be scared of directly addressing somebody's knee, their damaged hearing or their aching back, in case nothing happens. Then we really would feel foolish. Oh, there are so many questions!

Paul's first letter to the Corinthian church sums up exactly the weakness in the present day healing ministry in chapter two, from verse one. We can easily deduce from his writing what is missing. He says: 'When I came to you, brothers, I did not come with eloquence or superior wisdom as I proclaimed to you the testimony about God. For I resolved to know nothing while I was with you except Jesus Christ and him crucified. I came to you in weakness and fear, and with much trembling. My message and my preaching were not with wise and persuasive words, but with a demonstration of the Spirit's power, so that your faith might not rest on men's wisdom, but on God's power.'

In other words, he was coming from a place of great humility, not relying at all on his own ministry or his own knowledge — rather, he relied completely on the message of the cross to produce its own evidence of its own truth.

To think of the healing properties of the kingdom of heaven on earth is to think of heaven itself. There is a sense in which we all have numerous questions rumbling around in the backs of our minds, but we also know that, when we get there, all questions will fall away in the face of such beauty and holiness. To the potential 'kingdom walker' the situation becomes the same. As soon as the first step is over and done with, as soon as courage rises and another step out into the dry river bed seems possible, as soon as the waters begin to part and people begin to receive healing, it is then that our questions fade away into the background, blotted out by a driving thirst to go deeper, to know more, to see more, and to give more glory to the Lord.

Active 'kingdom walking', as I am trying to describe it in this book, is not a voice crying in the wilderness but a Christian life of discipleship. It is not a frothy idea floating around in the air, but feet on the ground going God's way. It is not an optional exotic plant, to be kept under glass and stared at out of interest, but it is a hardy perennial which bears twelve months of fruit in every kind of weather.

Nothing we can say or sing to God, no amount of speaking out all his wonderful names, is a valid substitute for the simple doing of his will. We may long for the beauty of eating bread with him in heaven, but this is wasted hope without our ploughing and planting in his kingdom here and now.

To think of him at his table but to forget him at ours is a bad investment. Learning kingdom theory from book or pulpit does not help the sick and the poor. There is no substitute for exploring every avenue of kingdom living, for their sake and for his. Any Christian with enough humility and courage is free to step into the river, to move out into the middle, so that thousands can walk safely past into the land of abundance that Jesus promised us through his words and works.

Although I draw my main picture from Joshua's river crossing adventures in the Old Testament, the truth about kingdom living is interlaced throughout the structure of the New Testament and the Old. Taking the two Testaments together, we see something amazing. Back in the garden of Eden, man and God conversed freely; there was peace and harmony. He is aware of all the damage sin has caused. The world is damaged by us, and we damage one another, but worst of all we are damaged by our experience of exile. We are in the wrong place and we are hurt. Thankfully, though, God has made it possible for us to be on intimate terms with him again; his will is to restore man to a state where there is no strife and sickness, nothing that can harm, and where we can enjoy fellowship with him. His prime motivation towards mankind, born out of the purest love for us, is restoration of a perfect relationship with him. Back before the bad days of disobedience, mankind received a considerable degree of God-given, delegated authority —to fill the earth and subdue it, to rule over the fish of the sea and the birds of the air, over the livestock, over all the earth, and over all the creatures that move along the ground. (See Genesis 1:28.) When God created the animals, he brought them to Adam for naming, such was the trust and friendship that existed. Then came that dreadful day when Adam disobeyed God and obeyed the enemy instead, and he and Eve lost what they had once enjoyed. Their disobedience meant that their delegated authority was gone.

So God sent Jesus, his only begotten Son, truly God and truly man, who would defeat Satan. Jesus then gave to his people a new commission, and that is why we believers are now a royal priesthood, a kingdom of priests. What do I mean by this? When Jesus left, he taught his disciples that all authority in heaven and on earth had been given to him. They were to go out into the world, make disciples, and teach them to obey everything he had commanded them. Amongst this wealth of instruction was the healing of the sick. They knew how to do it, and now they were given delegated authority again to do it.

The sick are healed because the kingdom of God is brought near to them; the sick and injured are restored to the Eden state of good health. But how can this be? How can the kingdom be revealed to a sickness? It happens because Jesus has delegated authority to us, showing others something of the kingdom.

To discover how we can do this, we can revisit Joshua and his adventures across the river into the promised land. Having got across the river Jordan he made camp outside Jericho. Joshua called the priests and ordered them, "Take up the ark of the covenant of the LORD and make seven priests carry trumpets in front of it." And he ordered the people, "Advance! March around the city, with the armed guard going ahead of the ark of the LORD." The seven priests carrying the seven trumpets went forward, blowing their trumpets, and the ark of the Lord's covenant followed them. They marched around the city once a day for seven days and then, on the seventh day, they marched around the walls seven times. One good shout and the walls came tumbling down! But how did they get the authority to organise such power? The clue is in the procession. In the front marched seven priests with seven trumpets. This is symbolic of praise and thanksgiving. Behind them, the object of their heralding, came the ark of the Lord, the word. The whole marching scene displayed an air of proclamation. This is a very different picture from prayer for healing such as is usually offered today.

In New Testament terms, praise and thanksgiving concentrated on the work of Jesus —as he is revealed in the Gospels, not perhaps the image we might have developed from our experiences as Christians. In Jesus, God reveals his saving power.

Praise to Jesus – and thanksgiving for what he has shown us and for what he has done – is irresistible. Praise and thanksgiving to him pulls back the curtain and reveals the kingdom. The Holy Spirit always glorifies Jesus, and he leads us to glorify Jesus in praise and thanksgiving —this is the heart of God, and as we praise and thank Jesus we align ourselves with his heart. The kingdom moves against the sickness at hand, and God's kingdom activity is revealed to the supplicant. Hell hates the sight and sound of this, and retreats. Christ has his way. The sick are restored.

***

Some fifteen years ago, living in Hong Kong, Margaret was spending some time at a theme park. She was relaxing in a big rubber ring and gently gliding down some water slides between small pools when a group of young men came down the waterslide behind her in tandem and crashed into her. Margaret was catapulted forwards and struck her head on the bottom of the pool when the ring she was on rotated forward. It took a number of weeks for the extent of the injury to become apparent. In essence, there was severe whiplash damage to the neck. Over subsequent years her neck did not heal, despite extensive medical investigation and treatment. The injury proved impossible to cure, and the best that could be achieved was palliative care for the reduced mobility, increasing pain, nausea and headaches.

In the mid-1990s Margaret also developed a 'frozen shoulder'. This compounded the difficulties because pain in one part of her upper body meant over-compensation from another part, which in turn became the next problem to be treated.

She had been able to receive a degree of divine healing, which increased the mobility in her neck and shoulder, and this enabled her to travel to London for a few days to receive treatment at a 'frozen shoulder' clinic.

For many years she could not shop by herself; she could not lift very much, and she was generally very restricted in terms of what she could do. She had to plan her route in the car as she was not able to make left turns without feeling nauseous. In an average week she would visit the physiotherapist at least once, and frequently more often than that. She was eventually diagnosed with irreversible neuro-tissue damage. She went from one mini-crisis to the next.

So Margaret learnt that her condition would be something she would have to live with. There were trips for treatment whenever her neck was out of alignment (leading to the severe headaches and nausea). She would often have to retreat to bed to lie down. She had to be very careful with everything she did, and the thought of how she would be in later years frankly frightened her.

We began to pray with her, much as we always do, and Margaret's neck began easing almost immediately. She felt the bones and muscles moving in her neck, back and shoulders; onlookers say that Margaret seemed to grow taller as her neck straightened.

She had been completely healed and made whole by the Lord Jesus. The lives of both Margaret and her husband, Phil, were transformed that weekend and, they feel, will never be the same again. Margaret can now do things she has not been able to do for over fifteen years, and she remains completely healed to this day. God's will was (as it is for every one of us who approaches Jesus with some expectancy) to see Margaret return to a life of abundance, the 'Eden state'.

What were the special words? How was it done? Whoever did the praying, how did they get that anointed? To find the answers we must go back again to the river Jordan and the approach to Jericho. What did the priests do there? They were the ones who took the risk with everything they knew and understood about God from their wilderness experiences. Then they stood in a very dangerous place where they might lose everything. That is what they did, and that is all they did.

God himself saw to it that the waters parted to make it easier for the people, but it was the people themselves who walked over. It was they who did the work. It was they who accepted the reality of the promise across the river —and had the courage to go for it!

It is the proclaiming, heralding, trumpet-blowing praise and thanksgiving by the priests that honours God and has the power to open doors to receiving healing. That is how it works. It has to be childlike and spiritually poverty-stricken, and it has to be built on a ready knowledge of all that Christ has indeed done for us during his life on earth, at the heart of which is Calvary.

The priests herald the coming of the living word. The act of praising and thanking Jesus for all he has done and all he has shown us proclaims the kingdom and brings it near.

It is as easy to see it this way: such simple, uncluttered expectancy draws the kingdom close; debate and cynical doubt push it away. Even debate about the nature of praise and thanksgiving can be an adverse pressure here —this would be like trying to split apart the light and the heat from a candle flame. It cannot be done without a real risk of extinguishing the flame.

But all is dependent on the speaking out of the good news of Christ, that he is our reliable and consistent Lord, Saviour and healer. We can tell it from the pulpit, we can read it out of the Scriptures, and we can re-tell it in our prayers of praise and thanksgiving, but it must be proclaimed.

I have heard that some interpret such an exhortation as our saying that if the gospel is preached, the sick will be healed. Of course the next easy step from that is to say, 'But I preach every Sunday morning and no one gets healed!', as if this then somehow negates the point. I am discovering something different. When the Bible speaks of 'preaching', the subject is always the same subject. The core material is always the dynamic proclamation of the good news of the kingdom of God— the poor in spirit are blessed, the repentant are forgiven by grace through faith in Christ crucified, and the sick are healed by the coming near of his kingdom.

So a kingdom walker is not someone who is in any way particularly gifted to heal – or to perform any other sort of miracle – he is someone who finds any sort of ways and means he can of preaching the good news of the kingdom, speaking of why it is good news and how it can be good news for the hearer. The Holy Spirit responds so richly. We are shown awesome deeds of righteousness from the Lord our Saviour, the hope of all the ends of the earth and of the farthest seas. Our times of trouble are crowned with his bounty; there is a great overflow of abundant life. The kingdom is released to us as good news. In the context of healing and miracle working, it is good news indeed that Jesus has taken all our pains and carried all our sickness, and that by his wounds we are healed.

Chapter Nine

ANY MORE PRIESTS, PLEASE!

In my mind's eye, there is a memory of holding a young lady's hands and feeling her nervously trembling. Her name is Laura. She feels a little scared and embarrassed so we offer to take her gently away from the glare of the platform lights and sit together with a colleague in the relative sanctuary of a shaded side aisle.

She is thirty years old, slim, elegant and utterly charming but has no feeling below her knees. She had contracted a viral infection when only a baby and had never been able to walk as she should or feel any sensation in her legs and feet. Balance had always been difficult, too —with no feeling in her toes she finds walking to be a clumsy trial although, after thirty years, she confesses she is getting used to it.

The muscles in her feet have atrophied over the years and bent her feet upwards, so the surgeons shortened her Achilles tendons a long while ago to flatten her feet onto the ground and make walking a little easier for her.

We sit and talk about Jesus and what his reactions to her would be if she had met him two thousand years ago. She struggles with the concept of his willingness to heal her as her churchgoing history is a history of unanswered prayer. So it seems we have to start again with her.

Quietly together, to avoid disturbing others at prayer, we give glory to God, remembering what Jesus has done for us on the cross. We magnify his name —that on Calvary he has made available all forgiveness and healing. I find it helpful to think of grace as being like the candle flame of the kingdom, forgiveness as being the light from that candle, and healing as the heat from its flame. Like all pictures, it is not perfect, it does not purport to be a doctrinally complete statement, and it needs to be qualified, but it expresses to me the heat of divine love for each of us, the way in which the light of Jesus is known in the release of forgiveness to the repentant sinner, and the way in which healing flows so readily in the life of the kingdom.

As we magnify his name, we do not do so mechanistically, nor in order to attempt to manipulate the kingdom (which is impossible anyway); and, in observing that in the life of the kingdom there is both forgiving and healing, we certainly do not suggest that those not yet healed are not forgiven. Rather, we simply honour God, praising and thanking him in the light of the good news of Jesus' sacrifice for us.

***

With a little encouragement, Laura got to her feet and walked a little way, and was soon bold and upright, with full balance restored. She came to see me the next day with the news that she had visited her doctor in the evening after we met, who confirmed that the tendons were now the naturally correct length, as they had been before surgery, and that full sensation had been restored to her legs and feet. She now walks, they tell me, in the style of the most elegant model that ever graced the front page of a fashion magazine.

Remembering her now, I am thinking back yet again to that first amazing, hesitant step the priests of Joshua took when the river parted. What a huge step for them! The river was in full flood; I wonder how it was that they did it? They may have wondered if they would lose everything they carried, or even take the risk of drowning. I wonder if one or two of them thought the exercise was pointless. Did anyone assume that all that could be gained might be nothing more than a group of wet priests? If Joshua were wrong in thinking that the waters might part for them but they did manage to swim across without nearly drowning, what would be there for them? Would there be anything especially different? Long ago, there had been reports of giants on the other bank, waiting to slaughter them, and cities with walls that went up to the skies. Of late things had looked better, as their latest spies claimed the whole country was in fear of them. Which spies were right? But what a risk! Surely it would be far more sensible to stay on the eastern bank with the Reubenites' families?

For most of us, the image of the God which we acquire from our experience is so entrenched in our belief system that we absolutely dare not let go. Unbelievably, our whole theology can be built on such a foundation.

Standing up in front of a group of listeners and telling them about the miracle working Jesus in the Gospels, the infinitely reliable and consistent one, provokes two extreme and by now quite predictable reactions from an audience or congregation. The reaction tends to be either extremely favourable, marked by contentment and joy, or extremely adverse, people wanting to run a mile from this. Why should negative reaction be as it is when one is preaching fully the good news of the kingdom of God? Two reasons spring to mind: firstly, most good teaching about the kingdom is just that —it is teaching and not preaching. There is a huge difference between these two, and miracles will hardly ever occur without the latter. Teaching is often presented in the form of a dry theological talk, rather than as good news expressed enthusiastically at street level. More on this later! Secondly, the leap from our prayer experience to New Testament fact is enormous, and may appear extremely unsafe. So much that we think we know and understand about God is based on our experiences. We tend to invest a great deal in what we think we have learnt from experience, so we have a great deal to lose. Experience, for many, seems to suggest that God does not heal everyone who prays, so we rationalise his apparent inactivity, devising spurious 'reasons' for what we think to be the case.

Like the priests carrying the ark and approaching the Jordan, we have to pick up all we know and take a giant step. We need to lean on the true, reliable Jesus of the New Testament. We shall know when we are doing so. Miracles of all sorts begin to happen around us and the rewards are incredible. So when we group together and speak out the scriptures about Jesus and express them in a simple form, the hearer may be thrilled by the immensity and the simplicity of the revelation, and want to plunge deeper into the river —or the mind may be working overtime to shut the ears tightly, so that they can hear no more.

We may not realise this, but those of us, and it is a large number, who have faith in a deity we have mentally constructed in our own image, coloured by our own disappointing experiences, will do battle at any and at all levels to hold on tightly to our belief position as if our very spiritual life is being threatened. This is often a battle taking place at a deep level, wherever and whenever miracles are seriously discussed or observed.

I would share this thought with all those who have a kingdom knowledge of the miraculous life: there are many sparkling days when hearers gasp at the simplicity of the message of the cross and its power —joyful days, when those whom we have taught are reporting that miracles of physical healing are beginning to happen around them too, and give glory to Christ. There are also what seems like more than my fair share of dark days, when all there appears to be in the church of this same Saviour is counter-argument while the sick go on in their suffering.

My whole raison d'être as a teacher is to beg the church, 'Will you take a risk for the sake of the sick, and do it for Christ?' But the silence of the response can sometimes be so disheartening! My simple, ordinary humanity sometimes tempts me into forgetting that this is not a matter for argument but a matter of the Spirit. If the opposite of frustration is patience, then I need patience with myself in all this, as well as with other people; with those who I am responsible for and those to whom I must give account, and with my peers; with those who love me and those who do not; in my mountain top experiences and in those almost incidental ones; in those unforeseen and sudden explosions of trouble, and under the weight of the daily valley-bottom grind; against disappointments; in all the times my heart breaks when those who should know better turn their backs on the restorative reasons for the shedding of blood at Calvary. Then again I need so much grace in the weariness of my mind and body, or the sometimes melancholic wearing down of my soul; in my own, only too sharp awareness of failure in my duty to Christ, or other people 'letting me down'. I need patience in my disappointments, losses, injuries, reproaches; in passing moods of heaviness in my heart, or that peculiar heart-sickness that attacks any of us in the middle of delayed hopes. I need it in all these things, from my childlike little troubles to what feels in the darker moments almost like the sufferings of a martyr, because I know that patience is the undiluted grace of God through which I can survive anything.

But every miracle given is a crown to carry to heaven for the King! I am often reminded that there was a time when Moses led Israel away and onwards from the Red Sea into the desert. For three days they went on in the merciless heat without finding anything to drink. When eventually they came to a small lake called Marah, they could not drink its water because it was bitter. As we might imagine, they complained, 'What are we going to drink?' Then Moses cried out to God in this emergency, and the Lord pointed out to him a piece of wood —a symbol in the Old Testament, signifying in advance the cross of Jesus. Prophetically, he threw it into the water, and the water became sweet. Would we expect anything to happen as a result of such an act? Most would think that such expectancy is unreasonable, unscientific, more than foolish. Yet my heart longs for God's people to have the courage to be in this sense 'foolish': willing to take a risk, put aside pride, pick up the cross, or rather its message, stop debating, and apply that simple heart of the message of the cross to someone else's sickness. More often than not, the results are of God — truly gracious.

If we take the kingdom step in easy stages it is very straightforward. Fighting off the voices of deliberate opposition, liberally laced with doubt, that are coming at us down the centuries is a far more difficult task.

1. Jesus' words teach us that the way to do the works is to believe [trust] in him. See John 6:28.
2. If we have faith [expectancy] and fight doubt we can move mountains. See Matthew 21:21f.

3. We all have a measure of faith [expectancy]; sometimes our faith is up and our doubts bring it down. See Romans 12:3.

4. Being left with a mustard seed of it at the end is sufficient. See Matthew 17:14ff.

5. Think again, the kingdom is close at hand. See Matthew 3:1f.

6. Preach the kingdom with boldness and enthusiasm, and give thanks for it and it will be revealed. See Mark 16:20 and Psalm 50:23.

7. When we reveal it, people get healed. See Luke 11:20.

It really could not be more simple, but we have to think about it! We doubt. We have alternative views. We say to ourselves, 'Anyone can throw a few scriptures together and make anything out of them!' We tell ourselves that it is wrong to raise the hopes of sick people, but Jesus himself teaches expectancy as a major key to receiving divine healing. We have different ways of thinking about it all, and the more we debate it because it does not fit our perception of God, or our understanding of divine healing, the further the kingdom floats away from the illness we would like to see disappear. It is only the childlike and the poor in spirit who will ever understand this. Our friends and our families suffer from disease and injury and we throw off the simple truth of the kingdom with extraordinary ease!

It must be that our belief system is quite fundamental to our personal power as people. Our self-power and our security are locked up in what we believe and we will fight to hold on to it, even in the face of such simple biblical truths. Meanwhile, although some among us might think of ourselves as pastors, we allow our flock to go on suffering, possibly quite unnecessarily.

I come across a starkly contrasting picture of this very battle on a weblog, a personal internet journal that is frequently updated and intended for general public consumption. One contributor wrote, after a time of kingdom teaching in his church:

'What a week we've had at our church. A week of healing, led by Mike Endicott. We witnessed miraculous healing, even I was used as an instrument of healing. Never before have I felt Jesus' power and presence more acutely. My theology has shifted over the past week

and I feel like a child in a candy store once again. I have gone all Jesus freaky! For too long we've been mushy, wishy-washy, cautious and 'intellectual' Christians who, when confronting suffering, pray that the 'victim' is comforted in their time of need. We have been so scared of praying for healing to a living, breathing, loving, risen Christ. Over this past week we did exactly that and many were healed. Tumours disappeared (x-ray evidence), lame walking out of their wheelchairs, literally hundreds of stories, miracles. [Read John 14:12-14.] I tell you the truth, anyone who has faith in me will do what I have been doing. He will do even greater things than these, because I am going to the Father. And I will do whatever you ask in my name, so that the Son may bring glory to the Father. You may ask me for anything in my name, and I will do it. The Gospels are littered with many such promises. Either these promises are empty ramblings by a madman or they are the Word of God. This past week we experienced the latter first hand. If we live in expectancy of these promises, God delivers.'

'Postmodernism will tell us to not read Jesus' words so literally. For too long I listened to that and I forgot that the Gospels are for simple people, not theologians, not philosophers, there is no need to explain away the absolute truth that exists for us in black and white. Christians have more reason to fear contrived, 'sensible', comfortable theology than anything other religions or secularism can throw at us.'

Another commentator, though, said that he was opting for 'a quiet, steady, consistent, relational, unspectacular ministry of inclusion.' It would be fair to say that the rift between such positions is more often seen amongst the leadership of the church than in the pews. To an extent the contrast can be between the pastoral and the apostolic impulse, both of which are vital in different ways. However we are not thinking here of those difficulties which can be surmounted by ordinary practical caring and human help, but of often desperate situations where prayer for the miraculous is offered, but then quickly set on one side as other approaches are pursued. The temptation of the pastor is to help all he can to make life comfortable for supplicants where they are. The apostolic tendency is to try to move them onwards and, hopefully, upwards. Many pastoral carers will enlist the support of any and all kinds of secular assistance to try to help (and there are many situations where that is perfectly proper and necessary), while the apostolic mind searches primarily for the supernatural intervention of God, drawing on divinely inspired Scripture concerning such things as expectant faith, signs and wonders. It is easy to see how the two callings sometimes seem to compete or conflict in ministry.

It seems that this potential 'rift' between the apostolic and pastoral impulses portrays a tension which needs some exploring. How can they enrich each other rather than 'compete'? I find this question close to a number of hearts. There are pastors who do not particularly want to resort to 'secular assistance', but who do long to pastor in the character and power of Christ.

Perhaps the analogy of Joshua's priests is a helpful one here, too. Let us imagine we have taken the first step and, to our immense pleasure and probably surprise, the waters have started to back up and people are starting to want to cross over in front of us. We still have a way to go, step by step out into the danger zone, until we reach the centre of the river bed. When we get there our role is to hold up the ark —in our terms, to proclaim the word of God, the wonders of the kingdom. That is what we do with physical healing needs, even when faced with that daunting water in front of us, representing in this picture the pile of people's problems with which we are confronted as we begin to minister in the kingdom work of healing.

Do we step out tentatively, or do we rush out confidently, with no fear of the waters facing us? Do we stand upright in the middle of the river bed, full of confidence that we are doing the right thing, or are we keeping a very wary eye on the water levels, in case they show even the slightest inclination to rise? —And if they do, are we ready to stand firm or to make a run for it?

The point is made. We should walk this road in the humility of our humanity, taking one step at a time, giving thanks for the fruit and gaining assurance as we go and, hopefully, eventually standing where we would like to be, right in the middle of it all and holding every difficulty at bay.

There is no sense here that God is to be tested, merely a complete reliance on his grace and his fatherhood to show us the way forward, gaining confidence in the message of the cross as we go.

The kingdom walker's real struggle is not against people, not against doubters and those with alternative views —it is a struggle against frustration, and for patience and grace. Once the walker has made it to the centre of the river there will be amazement over how easy it is! How simple it seems now to take the few small steps of obedience to Scripture that I have taken, and how earth-shattering were the revelations that came from that! One simple though almost impossible at the time, step —and thousands begin to receive the healing benefits of the promised land.

There will always be resistance to change, until we meet the Lord, and I have learned to repent of all the arrogance that held me defensively on the 'eastern bank'. But now I *know* that Jesus never said no when asked for what is clearly revealed as being in the Father's will; I know that he only did what he saw the Father doing, and that God never changes. It takes a mighty shrug to throw off the concept of God as slightly unreliable – a wrong concept, deriving from some kinds of misinterpreted experience – but I keep trying, and he keeps honouring me, and those I teach, with streams of healing miracles. These are not my empty and noisy, babbling boasts and bubbling promises, they are the promises of the character of God displayed in Jesus.

Chapter Ten

THE TROUBLE WITH DOUBT

Anne had badly twisted her left knee falling up a step, and she had reached a point of not being able to put her foot to the floor. That had become quite normal for her, as her legs had finished up at different lengths as she grew up. The knee was very swollen and felt to her as though it would break in half at any moment.

She had seen quite a few other people receive healing that same afternoon but secretly doubted very much that it would ever happen to her. She was prepared to accept that others might benefit from prayer but she had never done so herself before, and she knew no reason why God should start now.

So she wondered if she should ask initially for some much smaller blessing, perhaps the calming down of her slight headache, but after a great deal of hesitation (and friendly words from members of her family along the pew) she felt the urge to ignore her doubts and jump into the river of God's grace pouring through the kingdom and ask for complete healing for her inflamed joints and the lengthening of her right leg.

After a little time of prayer and thanksgiving for the cross, she found herself down on her knees in prayer and adoration, something for which she had not had the ability or the inclination for quite a while. Both knees had received healing.

The next day she still had to use two crutches, the following day one, and since then none —the swelling had gone right down; her leg had lengthened, she was bending again quite comfortably and the knee was back to normal. The following Sunday she testified in church to her healing, to encourage the others further. This was not such a difficult thing to do as everyone could see that she had stood unaided in the music group for most of the service.

So our next step out towards the middle of the river bed must be to understand at least some little measure of the power of doubt to draw us back to the 'eastern bank' from where we stepped out in the first place. It troubled Anne and it troubles us, too. She imagined from her past experience that healing was for other people, but that thought does not match the Jesus revealed in Scripture —he never refused anyone. So she had some alternative thought about him. She had a doubt.

Now it is most important in kingdom working that we understand this word we are using, 'doubt'. There are two kinds of religious doubt: unbelief which questions the character and deity of Jesus – that sort of doubt is sinful – and the problem of misunderstanding that we are discussing in these pages, which is error. They are very different from each other, which is why the original Greek throughout the New Testament uses a word in connection with the working of miracles which is best translated as meaning 'an alternative way of thinking'. For example, we are constantly exhorted in the Bible to have faith and not to doubt. This indicates that we should have expectancy of Jesus to do miraculous things when we ask, as he told us he would, and not have such alternative views as 'anyone else, but probably not me', when Jesus is 'yes' and 'amen' to all who come to him for healing.

The thought that this might not apply to Anne for some unknown reason, 'Well, probably not today, anyway,' is an alternative thought, a misunderstanding of the will of God, a mistake.

Thinking of another case altogether, I remember a young teenage girl who dragged her reluctant mother to the front of the queue. "Can you help my mum?" she asked me most politely. "She has a very bad back and she's had it for years!"

I looked questioningly at mum and she confirmed her daughter's diagnosis with a nod. The daughter went on, "She wouldn't come up on her own as she thinks she's insignificant." She smiled, lovingly.

"Mum," I chided her, "there is no such word as 'insignificant' in the kingdom. Anyway, God thinks you are worth dying for!"

I took her hands and began to give glory for the cross. Careful but rigorous physical activity a short while later proved her complete healing.

These are clear examples of how thoughts alternative to the image of God portrayed by Christ can rule our perception of – and our relationship with – God, and be a block to our receiving.

These misunderstandings that we call doubts are far and away the worst block of all. We may study and contemplate interminably all sorts of other blockages to receiving healing, but we will never find another one anything like as powerful as this kind of doubt. All the others added together do not interfere with the flow of grace like this one!

Cynicism, scepticism and the debating of alternative ideas about miracle working (i.e. contrary to those taught and displayed by Jesus) are all, in this context, doubt. Reverent enquiry into the meaning of Scripture is one thing, cynicism or procedural scepticism are quite different from that. To elucidate the contrast, imagine two people strolling through a wood in springtime, who both catch sight of a high bird's nest. Both are sufficiently intrigued to want to take a closer look at the eggs. We might think of a kingdom walker as being like one who takes a risk, climbs the tree and strains out along the branch to peer into the nest, taking the greatest care to ensure that the subject matter remains intact. We could think of the doubter as one who cuts down the tree to bring it closer to himself, destroying both the nest and the eggs in the process.

We need to be continuously and honestly aware of any doubts (alternative thinking) about the kingdom, and the effects of those doubts on our Christian walk before we can truly be free to explore the kingdom. Jesus' teaching consistently shows us that expecting is a major catalyst in the kingdom's restorative work, and that doubt (not only as unbelief, but alternative views of God's will), tends to destroy that expectancy. If people did but realise it, alternative thinking about the kingdom, wondering if God will answer healing prayer and making excuses for him when he appears not to, soon turns the world around us into a spiritual desert, in which we do not hear God speak, nor sense divine footsteps —we fail to perceive his hand at work in our lives.

So we need to remind ourselves often that unbelief in the sense we have considered is a sin. In the whole area of healing and miracles, doubting signifies holding onto some alternative way of thinking about a biblical kingdom principle. Such doubting usually results from the teaching of poor healing theology, or life's experiences, contradicting a kingdom principle expressed in the words and works of Jesus —even if the doubter has no working knowledge of the principle involved.

Kingdom living includes walking deeper and deeper into a triumph of expectancy over doubt. It does not, of course, mean we will never make a mistake. Thinking of oneself as being unfit to receive from God, as many do for a huge variety of reasons, is not evil, it is a mistake. Believing that some current bout of illness is a punishment sent from God is not sinful, it is merely incorrect. The church's teaching for many centuries that suffering in old age is God's way of soul purification before death is not a sin but a total mistake.

When it comes to understanding our relationship with God and the healing ministry, we are all disciples in the making. We are limited, grappling with things that are simply too high for us. Obviously we human beings, even at our best, will still make many mistakes, but making mistakes in our understanding of God's intent need not necessarily be sinful.

Our actions are generally coloured by a combination of our motives, intelligence and conditioning: our intentions may be very good, but because our mental capacity is limited, the action, or resultant spiritual understanding, may turn out to be mistaken —but not necessarily sinful, because culpable sin arises out of wrong intention. Therefore alternative (unbiblical) views, taught over the centuries by poor healing theology (e.g. God might not want to heal us) and our experiences and circumstances (which might only serve to cement the wrong teaching), may carry a definite sense of disappointment, incompleteness and frustration —but they need not leave a person feeling guilty.

Kingdom living, having expectancy about the outcome of prayer, does not mean perfect living in the sense of living without flaw or error, but it does mean aiming for a simple and an obedient life —and that can still be consistent with our making many mistakes. If we are really being open to the work of the Holy Spirit, he will be guiding us into all truth, leading us to repent of whatever ways in which we have fallen short of God's best will and purpose, and always drawing us back to Jesus who is himself the truth.

Our ability to perform miracles and to receive them is directly tied into our net expectancy. If we subtract our alternative ways of thinking from our positive expectancy and the result is negative (or at the very most still less than the size of a mustard seed) then we do not receive. Most of the church today is in a negative position, unable to see the kingdom and unable to receive many of its restoring benefits.

In Anne's case, for example, she was not aware of the kingdom principle that the river of God's grace flows constantly into the world where we are. It makes no individual decisions about us since Calvary, it simply flows all over us. It flows with equal vigour over sinners and the righteous alike, male and female, holy and unholy, Christian or otherwise.

Anne began by thinking otherwise out of her past experiences —but, since her healing, not now! Being in two minds on this topic, as she used to be, interferes with our being able to receive our inheritance, the riches of Calvary stored up for us in the kingdom. As we minister for healing in the kingdom, we find that, through his grace, God is generously pouring down kingdom riches to everyone who comes to Jesus, without first finding fault with them. He never lays down conditions for the gift. More fruitful answers do not come from the clearing away of obstacles. But when we ask we must trust and not doubt, because when we doubt we are like a wave on the surface of the sea, blown and tossed about by the wind. We become double-minded people, unstable in all we do and should not necessarily expect to receive anything from the Lord. (See James

1:5-9.) Imagine trying to stand upright in a fishing boat on a high running sea while trying to catch a tennis ball!

A common example of these unbalancing soul disturbances might be the Christian who, on the one hand, believes that God loves everyone to the same degree and wishes to see all healed (or would simply love to believe it), but also believes from sheer experience, that healing prayer is a hit and miss thing, sometimes working, most often not working —and that the supplicant, and maybe the minister, may never have seen a miraculous healing in their entire lives. They may have heard of one or two, but cynically suspect there may well have been other medical or psychological reasons for the healing instead. (There may have been, but all things come from God.) One view says that Jesus is Lord, Saviour and healer, while the other view agrees but wonders if it will work out in practice. These two views oppose each other, but both are often held in the same person's mind at the same time.

I describe doubt as being the largest and most effective blockage to the would-be kingdom walker. There are many questions about the miraculous that readily present themselves on the surface, but two main faults underlie all those 'double-minded' (being in two minds about something) cracks in our expectancy. The first, as we observed, is cynicism. This is a particularly Western European trait, possibly arising from both religious history and often the phenomenon of incomplete conversion to Christianity. It has antecedents in ancient philosophies which enjoin submitting to an inevitability of things, and sadly it is found in the church today. Hence we hear expressions such as: 'these things are sent to try us', and, 'worse things happen at sea', 'old age does not come on its own', and, 'what will be, will be.' The second great interference in the flow of miraculous and heavenly grace has to do with our exaltation of science. It readily offers alternative ways of thinking. This is an easy road down which to slip unknowingly into idolatry: easy, because human nature is inclined to believe only what can be understood or explained. If healing cancer seems like a higher mountain to climb than healing the common cold it is because it is so for science. Not so in the kingdom.

There is a sense in which this sorry state of affairs is quite understandable. Our medical practice is seen as a door through which we might find, on those occasions when we need it, a world that has clear scientific and natural laws which can be used to powerful effect by those charged with their distribution. Sadly, it can no longer be said that the church is a door through which we ought to find, on those occasions when we need it, a kingdom that has clear dynamics, spiritual and holy laws which may be used to powerful effect by ministers.

Medical practice knows a great deal about how its world works, and tries its utmost to benefit those in need of it. The church knows little of – and has even less expectation of – how its kingdom works at street level, and therefore has little real expectation of benefiting those in need of that kingdom.

So the kingdom walker must always be on guard against doubting a word or promise from the Bible, and of avoiding the perfect and reliable image of God portrayed by Jesus, simply because it does not match his life's experiences or he does not understand it! Such thought patterns reduce God to the level of our minds, not allowing for his acting in our bodies, and so reducing the level of faith in our souls.

So we need to look further at this interfering factor of doubt, consider some of its major causes, and see how the truth of Jesus can deal with such a blockage.

Chapter Eleven

DEFEATING THE ENEMY

Katie wheeled herself up to the front of the platform and we jumped down to be with her.

"What do you want us to pray for?" I asked her. It would always be wrong to start by assuming that people who ride in wheelchairs see walking as their prime need at that moment, and this was true now.

"I don't expect to get out of my chair, but it would be really nice if I could feel my toes move," Katie responded with a grin.

The person appointed by the organisers to work with me that evening said, kindly and gently, "Don't expect too much, Katie, God doesn't want to heal everyone, you know."

'Oh dear,' I thought, under my breath. 'That simply isn't true! The last thing we need is doubt being pumped into the situation here. Of course God wants to heal everyone who comes to Jesus with a mustard seed of expectancy —did not Jesus display that over and over again in his earthly ministry? Did he not then emphasise that he and the Father are one? Not one was refused.'

I asked the person assisting me to be kind enough to go backstage and search for two bottles of drinking water for us. I was not in the least thirsty but remembered both Jesus and Peter clearing the room when raising the dead to remove too much alternative thinking from the scene.

Then I told Katie about Jesus, that he never refused anyone who came to him with expectancy as small as a mustard seed, and that nothing, absolutely nothing, could come between her and the love of God. I boldly shared with her, in other words, some of the good news of Jesus and his miraculous kingdom and the power of the message of the cross. Her toes began to wiggle. Her expectancy rose even more. "In that case," she wondered, "what about my knees?"

And so we went on. As the healing moved up her legs so her expectancy rose further in her heart. In fifteen minutes or so her broken back was mended and she was pushing her wheelchair away from the platform, shaking with joy and tears and praising God.

Now there are many degrees of growth in the area of 'alternative thinking' and unbelief about kingdom matters, as the assistant was displaying before going off to hunt for water. Here are some of them.

Firstly, some of us simply lack the confidence to come to God and receive from him, through simple and childlike trust, the rich abundance of heaven that we need in our particular situation. We find that we cannot joyfully or easily 'draw water from the wells of salvation' (Isaiah 12:3), but keep ourselves a little at a distance, wanting to approach and yet not risking it.

Secondly, we are prone to forget our absolutely concrete status as kingdom beneficiaries (always supposing that we have indeed been taught that joyful truth in the first place). The possibility of inheriting and receiving the restoring benefits of the kingdom – as heirs, as children of our heavenly Father – start to fade when we cannot sing out with an overflowing heart,

> Surely God is my salvation;
> I will trust and not be afraid.
> The LORD, the LORD, is my strength and my song;
> he has become my salvation.
>
> *Isaiah 12:2*

Thirdly, matters begin to deteriorate rapidly when we begin to seriously question Christ's willingness and ability to supply such kingdom riches as miraculous gifts of healing. At this point we cannot go to him for our own needs any more. We may still be able to intercede for others, but not in any serious spirit of expectancy for ourselves or for them. This is more or less where Katie had got to over the godly promise of healing, displayed through the life of Jesus, for her broken back.

From then on, things can begin to speed up on their way downhill when we question whether it is right to expect anything from God in some particular circumstance. At this point we often work up many apparently sound but really pseudo-biblical arguments – the old one about the manipulation of God, or about some being especially favoured – to maintain this state of unbelief, and justify hanging back from Christ.

If at this point we are still looking secretly to Jesus and into the kingdom at all, it is probably with a glutinous, negative mixture of expectancy and alternative thoughts: that we will probably not be any better off for having asked, sought and knocked. This unbelief can eventually grow to the point where we decide that our situation will probably not be particularly interesting to the Lord, perhaps even concluding that, although our case is desperate, it will not be redeemable by him. It feels as though we might be cut off, as we read in Ezekiel 37:11,

> Then he said to me: "Son of man, these bones are the whole house of Israel. They say, 'Our bones are dried up and our hope is gone; we are cut off.'"

Our general level of trust in the image of the reliable and consistent miracle working Christ revealed in Scripture may grow even less from here, manifesting itself in our sharing with (or even teaching) our doubts to other people in ways that tear down kingdom principles and working – to the great scandal of the godly – to the dishonour of God. We tell others, for example, that Christ does not wish to see everyone healed who asks him with a mustard seed of expectancy, an untruth about the kingdom which only serves to pump doubt into the church and keep the sheep from their healer. Even worse, we can find ourselves questioning all the promises of God. With David, we may be crying out that all men are liars (see Psalm 116:11), but unlike David we may be losing any practical awareness of the faithfulness and reliability of God. Some people then have so much doubt and alternative thought swollen up inside them that they proclaim the Gospels to be nothing other than a pile of delusion and a sweet set of stories of legend. Sadly, we can reach the end: we can come to question whether there is indeed a living, loving, personally-relating, restoring God who rules. These doubts are dreadful degrees of blockage to our receiving, and to enjoying God's will, and they will make the wholesome kingdom walker's flesh creep.

So where does all this sort of doubt come from? Anyone setting out to walk humbly in the kingdom should be very aware of these things as they may well arrive unannounced and, without testing, be unrecognised. There are two fountains that readily supply us with alternative thoughts, ideas that run contrary to the image of God portrayed by Jesus: Satan, and man himself.

Firstly, Satan's active hand moves like this— he provokes us to measure God's healing grace by our own experiences rather than by the Jesus of the Gospels, the perfect image of the invisible God. Satan cannot afford for us to see the truth, for if we catch a glimpse of the real Jesus at the heart of the kingdom we begin at once to give glory to God for the work of the cross, something Satan finds most unwelcome! From using our own experience as the benchmark, we may develop a tendency to be dismissive of the miraculous works of God, of his loving us, and of all his ways. Our dismissive conclusions are then reinforced and scepticism grows. Having gained some momentum here, the enemy works on our naturally wicked hearts with very great effect, so that we start questioning the truth of the Lord and his word, and of course giving up hope of help and healing for ourselves and for others. We may continue to pray for the sick, but more out of impatient duty than excited certainty. Now he tries to drive the soul away even further, filling it with a minefield of tiny prejudices against God and his gloriously simple kingdom truths and realities. At this point Satan will represent God as being one who is usually distant, certainly unreliable, preferring one person to another, and varying each day in his level of concern with our daily life. When this is done, it is then easy for him to fill the Christian's mind with alternative thoughts and his mouth with untrue sayings that pull down both the kingdom and those who proclaim it. Such ideas would include God having other plans than seeing the supplicant healed, a mystical sense of timing (which allows the minister to excuse apparent delay), and the unbiblical thought that suffering from bad health or injury might be good for us.

It is now relatively easy for Satan to darken our understanding even further, so that we will not see the glory of the gospel or the covenant of grace. These things become wisps of mist to us. Neither will we be able to realise the shining lustre and beauty of holiness and the riches of the kingdom waiting for us. In fact, Satan actually helps the Christian to work out, and speak out, all sorts of prejudices against other people's right to inherit those same riches, because that person has little real hope of receiving any of those benefits for themselves. From here it is a simple step down to the place of questioning all godly things, and the assumption that they are all mere delusions. We are now only one step away from atheism.

However, Satan cannot be blamed for everything here. There are also a number of sinful causes of doubt within the Christian heart. Pride and haughtiness of mind, thinking that our own strength is worth relying on, is one of them. (See Psalm 30:7.) Self-confidence, pride's brother and companion, encourages us to step out in our own strength rather than in the Spirit's power. We can easily fall into the muddy whirlpool of doubt by failing to watch our own deceitful hearts which keep us standing off at a distance from the living God. (See Hebrews 3:12.) This often works by our readily giving in to doubting and questioning thoughts very early on our kingdom adventure. It is not honouring to the Lord to sit down and discuss things with Satan! Eve's way of doing this very thing should serve as a warning to us.

Again, it is too easy to lose touch with our own wants, and with our everyday need of Christ, and to forget to use our own faith to pray over and into such things. When our mustard seed of faith expectancy is not used it can become rusty and weakened, and eventually lost.

When we no longer delight each other, and ourselves, by thinking about Christ and pleasurably talking about his work of restoration and redemption, about the gospel and its promises, these things tend to lose their beauty and glory in the soul. They lose the lustre they once had, and this loss opens a door to both human and demonic mischief.

So how can the places lost to doubt be reclaimed? How do we begin to switch back to the right image of God? We begin by reminding ourselves that Jesus is the author and perfecter of our faith, and just as, in the Gospel stories, he rebuked unbelief, he can do it again. He is the great teacher, bringing understanding of the gospel, bringing abundant life to light through it, and revealing its beauty again.

The Jesus revealed by Matthew, Mark, Luke and John brings all the promises of God home to the soul, vitally alive in their absolute reality, perfection and truth, confirming those promises of God so that they are all 'yes' and 'amen' in him. This effectively establishes expectancy in the heart, and throws doubting and alternative thoughts out of the mind.

The reliable and correct key to defeating doubts and alternative thinking about the kingdom and its reliable and consistent King is 2 Corinthians 10:3-5,

> For though we live in the world, we do not wage war as the world does. The weapons we fight with are not the weapons of the world. On the contrary, they have divine power to demolish strongholds. We demolish arguments and every pretension that sets itself up against the knowledge of God, and we take captive every thought to make it obedient to Christ.

So the kingdom does not advance because we fight and attack anything that we imagine might be getting in the way of it. But we have been given a method which has the divine power to demolish strongholds, so long as we can correctly identify a stronghold for what it is. The strongholds which effectively prevent the church from displaying the kingdom to the world are man's philosophical arguments against the full and abundant flow of supernatural grace, and every image of God to which we might give credence that is contrary to the image of God displayed through Jesus according to Scripture. We can overcome our wrong images, little by little, by taking captive every single alternative thought and comparing it with the grace and truth of our Lord himself.

The Holy Spirit blows away the mists of doubt that cloud our view of the kingdom as we push away false images of God derived both from our experience and also from alternative ideas —replacing them with the truth as we study Jesus, whose will and purpose are revealed in Scripture.

Chapter Twelve

KINGDOM PRAYER

Mary stood in front of the sympathetic crowd gathered around her and briefly explained the dreadfulness of fibromyalgia. She told us: "It is a disease that affects the nerves and muscles in the body; nerves become inflamed, causing extreme muscle pain, nerves and muscles hurting and burning at the same time."

Mary's pain began at the base of the neck, radiating down the shoulders, arms, hips and buttocks, continuing down through the legs and calves. Her muscles were tight and drawn and painful, burning and hurting continuously. The disease is not life-threatening, but her life was ruined by it.

As we began to give thanks for the finished work of the cross, her pain began to dissolve, first down the left hand side and then down the right. As it finally all left her, she confessed (as others have been heard to do so before) being left with the sensation of a warm blanket around her neck. Immediately, another Mary in the congregation exclaimed, "Me, too!" While sitting listening to the first Mary, she too had been busy receiving healing for a strong dose of osteoarthritis. Her pain had all disappeared as well. The two Marys had simultaneously 'breathed in' the kingdom and found the riches that they needed. We had pressed into it and found God to be pressing down towards us in his love and his readiness to see kingdom restoration prevail.

Two days later the fibromyalgia returned. Mary was in agony again but this time things were going to be different. She remembered that I had told her that healing is like salvation —once received, not lost. She recalled that I had given to her the teaching of John 10:10 that Jesus had come to give her an abundant life and that the enemy had come to kill and to steal and destroy. If symptoms recur, often this is not a loss of healing as such, nor a sliding back into sin or anything of the kind. The most likely cause is that the enemy is trying to convince the person that the cross has not worked in this particular case. It is very much in the devil's interest to deny the victory of the cross in any way he can, and to return the symptoms. So she did exactly as I suggested: she addressed the pain directly, and told it not only to go but to go back where it came from! Twenty four hours later her peace returned and the illness never troubled her again.

She told it to go? Where did she get that authority from? Kingdom walkers, disciples who have walked into the middle of the river, must be prepared to be warriors in prayer, and teach others to be as well. Mary's actions at this point were all to do with prevailing in battle. We need to know that doing spiritual battle is vital for the kingdom to be revealed in miraculous ways; it can be the deciding dynamic. The spiritual battlefield the kingdom walker is concerned with is the whole earth. Ultimately, the war has to do with the dominion of this planet (and everyone of us who lives here) —it will be manifestly ruled by Christ, and everything will be seen to be placed under his feet, but in the meantime it is a spiritual battleground. As every Christian will happily declare, the rightful King over all things is Jesus, the Son of God and the world's Creator, but there is a pretender, described in Scripture as the 'god of this world', who is working against him and attempting to usurp his throne. This enemy, Satan, has been trying to hold onto the kingdom for himself and overthrow the rightful ruler, by the use of various underhand tactics. Wherever the kingdom is pushed to one side by such things as sickness and disease, there we see one part of the local struggle being temporarily lost.

I would not wish to suggest here that all sickness is demonic – that would not be true – but Jesus says that the enemy has come to steal and to kill and to destroy, and that is exactly what sickness does to us.

But the rightful King, Jesus, using an utterly different way – of love and persuasion – seeks to win the world back to its first loyalty and to open again, as it were, the gates of Eden. When God saw, in the first place, what and whom he had made in Eden, he said that it was 'good' and 'very good'. Jesus' sacrifice has torn the curtain in the temple, opening the gates that lead to an abundant life on earth. (See again John 10:10.)

Jesus fought a fierce three year battle on earth with the pretender, Satan, and, after a consistent succession of victories, achieved the great conquering triumph of the cross and resurrection. There is, we should notice, one peculiar side to this victory which makes it different from any stereotypical example of the military kind of victory. A decided victory, and the complete conquest of the general officer commanding the enemy troops, has not put an end to hostilities. We might naturally expect that, according to normal military protocol, the enemy would have surrendered on the first Easter morning, or at least agreed to an armistice, but it has not happened. The reason for this is extraordinary. Our conquering Christ has a deep love for us —longing to win his way into our hearts with our unrestricted invitation to do so. So the war has been left open for our sake. It goes on and on; a thousand battles each await our response to that love.

When the time eventually came for God to implement the great climax of his strategic plan to save the world, he himself came down as man, in the person of Jesus. His time here on earth is the blueprint for kingdom praying; the dynamic movement of his earthly ministry demonstrates the movement and effect of kingdom prayer. He came down, he won the victory, he returned to heaven. The gifts flowing from the victory of Calvary include forgiveness, peace, abundance, eternal life, healing, a new nature and a robe of his righteousness. For further reading about the gifts of Calvary please see my book entitled *Heaven's Dynamite*, specifically the chapter entitled The Heart of the Matter.

So in kingdom praying there is no need to discern God's will for a given situation. We pray in the light of any and all of the above listed gifts, already given on Calvary. We can consider the problem, think of the relevant Calvary gift, and pray. Then we will always be praying directly into the will of God. Discernment is not necessary here, his will has already been revealed concerning all healing matters.

It is so important, while praying kingdom prayers, that we are most attentive to the problem at hand. We must study it enough to allow compassion to flow, using the six gifts as a checklist keeping us aware of the available grace. We must pray with a simple, childlike expectancy that what we are asking for is on its way. And in all this there is to be praise, worship and thanksgiving.

Effective kingdom prayer always begins in heaven in God's heart, enters into a human heart in the battle, intersecting the space between the two —which is the real battlefield of prayer. Then it returns again to where it started, in joyful thanksgiving, having carried out the divine purpose. It is like the movement described in Isaiah 55:11,

> "...so is my word that goes out from my mouth: It will not return to me empty, but will accomplish what I desire and achieve the purpose for which I sent it."

His word comes, achieves and then returns. So it is with kingdom prayer. While Daniel was praying, confessing both his sin and the sin of Israel, and making his petition to the Lord for his holy hill, the angel Gabriel flew swiftly to see him at the time of the evening sacrifice. He said,

> "Daniel, I have now come to give you insight and understanding. As soon as you began to pray, an answer was given, which I have come to tell you, for you are highly esteemed."
>
> *Daniel 9:22f.*

The spiritual battle for the restoration of Jerusalem had already begun before Daniel became aware of it. Later, the angel appears to Daniel and tells him,

> "Since the first day that you set your mind to gain understanding and to humble yourself before your God, your words were heard, and I have come in response to them. But the prince

of the Persian kingdom resisted me twenty-one days. Then Michael, one of the chief princes, came to help me, because I was detained there with the king of Persia."

Daniel 10:12f.

The angels Michael and Gabriel had already been fighting a three week long battle in Persia before Daniel began to understand that his prayers had even been heard. We can watch this dynamic again when God tells Elijah,

"Leave here, turn eastward and hide in the Kerith Ravine, east of the Jordan. You will drink from the brook, and I have ordered the ravens to feed you there."

1 Kings 17:3f.

God's will came first; his doing – organising the ravens – had already taken place before any action was required on Elijah's part. Provision for the prophet's sustenance had already been made before he set out.

The conclusion of the Lord's Prayer – "For thine is the kingdom, the power and the glory…" – reminds us that the whole movement of kindom miracle working is always an act of God's firm will being despatched in heaven, actioned on earth in power, the results provoking our hearts into returning glory, praise and thanksgiving. One major reason why miracle-working kingdom prayer is so effective is because it is certain of this dynamic, and the prayer-giver's role within it.

Now, prayer is the common generic term used to describe all our dealings with God. I must always take care to remember, within that definition, that kingdom praying comes in three distinct parts: communion, petition and intercession. The first type of prayer, and far and away the most important one in the kingdom, is communion, simply being on good terms with God. It involves the cross (the kingdom's epicentre) as the basis of my coming near, getting close and being on good terms with him. This means that it involves my coming to God through the crucified body of Jesus, the Christian's way through to the Holy of Holies. This communion means my having fellowship with him, it is not my asking for those things I need and cannot get for myself or for other people; it simply means enjoying him, thinking about him, loving him, delighting in how beautiful and wise, capable and loving he is, being with him without any words. Every kingdom walker should constantly practice the habit of inwardly gazing on God. As someone who has experienced rebirth, I know that something inside my heart can 'see' God. Even when I find I have to pull back my attention in order to get on with earthly matters, there is still a secret communion always going on between us. This is the truest way that I can worship him, thinking how worthy he is of all the best of everything I could possibly bring to him, and a great deal more than that. It has to do with my relationship with him being right. As in the example of Daniel, it includes confession of sin on my part, out of necessity, and receiving his forgiveness. This is the only way, as we have already seen, into proper fellowship with him.

Adoring and worshipping (not merely the performance of hymn singing) belong to this first phase as well. Communion like this is the fundamental basis of all prayer as far as the kingdom explorer is concerned. It is the absolutely vital breathing in and out of the true miracle working Christian life. It concerns the two of us, God and me. It yields a growing, confident knowledge of that solid relationship with him.

Consider Elijah, a man just like us, on Mount Carmel. To show the absolute reality of the true God and his kingdom he built an altar. Those false prophets, in opposition to him, did so as well. When the opposition had failed to elicit any fire from heaven (because their gods were false and inactive), Elijah soaked his altar and bull with water and then set out to receive that miracle from the true God, with a confidence in the outcome which was nothing short of staggering. The fire came down and consumed the sacrifice.

However, Elijah's proof of the reality of God did not work effectively because of attention to ritual or quality of prayer or submission to correct ecclesiastical processes and procedures. His miracle worked for him as he had expected because he knew it would. Jesus spoke of 'trust' or 'faith', which we can take as signifying such a sense of certitude, practical confidence that God will act. In the case of Elijah, we think of the months and years spent alone with God in deserts and wildernesses and lonely places, in tight communion with him. Elijah did not waste the time on the mountain trying to work out the best way to maximise his chances of success. Things happened because he knew they would. Too many believers have a 'hit and miss' experience of prayer —they keep going because they must, but the results are often unreliable. The cause is simple – insufficient communion (meaning here real fellowship with God). The second form of prayer is petition, in its narrower significance of asking something for oneself. This is made up of definite requests to God for things we need. Our entire life is totally dependent on God's riches and his generous hand. Everything good comes from him. Our friendships, health and strength, our ability to make money, help of many kinds – bodily, mental and spiritual – all these things come from God, and require our being constantly in touch. We have to keep the door open between God and us; he opened it long ago with the cross of Christ. Again, we recall that our whole prayer life, including petition, hinges on continual personal communion with our wonderful God.

The third form of essential kingdom prayer is intercession. True prayer never stops with petition for the things we need for ourselves, it reaches out for other people. The very word intercession implies a reaching out; it means standing as a mutual friend, between God and someone who is perhaps out of touch with him, or who might need some special kind of help. It is the climax and outward drive of prayer.

We could think of communion and petition as being both upwards and downwards. Intercession can only exist with any effective power when it is the natural flowing outworking of these other two kinds of prayer.

In all these different movements of prayer, in all true prayer in the kingdom, the Holy Spirit is at work, and our communion, petitions and intercessions are prompted by the Spirit, enabled by the Spirit and led by the Spirit. If our prayer is truly kingdom prayer, arising from the life of the kingdom (marked by that faith and obedience we have already discussed), then it is he who first convicted us of sin, showed us our need, led us to repent and receive Christ, and gave us new birth. When the Spirit of Christ is at work in us, then our prayer is kingdom prayer, and is Spirit-led, whether or not it is expressed in words. With God thus at work in us, his life active in us through the presence and operation of the Holy Spirit, there are profound effects in us —and as we interact with other people. He can now use us: in us, his kingdom impacts others.

***

Annette came wearily up to us at the end of a long day and a long healing service. "I have a lot of trouble with my feet. I always have done for as long as I can remember. The muscles are all twisted and knotted and very painful."

The single word 'Now' arrived in the back of my mind. "What are they like now?" I enquired of her.

"When I go shopping I have to sit down after half an hour, the pain is too great to bear!"

"Yes, but what are they like now?" I wondered if she had heard me.

"They are absolute agony after we have been standing a long time in church…"

"Yes," I repeated myself, "but what about *now*?"

She stopped talking for a moment and looked down at her feet. Then she looked up at me again and said sheepishly. "Oh, how embarrassing!" She had been healed. There was no intercession prayer needed. All had been done through communion and the proclamation of the good news of Christ as healer. The kingdom surrounded and enveloped her feet, and all was glory to Christ.

So, communion and petition cement and continue my relationship with God, preparing me for outreaching intercession. Kingdom prayer has to begin with the first two but reaches its climax in the third. I need that certain touch with God. I must have constant petition and receiving, but the true kingdom adventurer's heart absorbs the warmth of the heart of God and reaches out hungrily for the world. In doing this, in working miracles to reveal the kingdom of God on earth, we will constantly be watching defeat after defeat by the persistent kingdom praying of someone in whom the Lordship of Jesus and the life of the Spirit are present and active. Every time such a person prays, the blood-dyed flag of Jesus Christ is waved over Satan's head, and the enemy must flee.

Every kingdom walker who gives himself to kingdom prayer is used by God as a new position in the battleground, where Jesus' victory banner is flown. The kingdom walker is God's foothold in enemy occupied territory. And the Holy Spirit at work inside that person, on that new spot of holy ground, will persistently insist on the enemy's retreat in the name of Jesus the Lord, Saviour and healer. This is how the kingdom walker attends to prayer.

Chapter Thirteen

AND OUT INTO THE MIDDLE

To continue a little further with our extended metaphor, like Joshua's priests we have walked out into the middle of the river, having taken what we imagine we know about heaven's healing grace, the church's ministry of healing, everything we think we know about the God of restoration and his kingdom, having been prepared to lose any and all of it that might have been derived from a mistaken image of him. Mysteriously, the water splits in two and there is a strip of more or less dry ground for those who wish to do so to walk across. From now on it is all about how the people are going to respond to the potential of the promised land.

Some will always wish to stay with the Reubenites' livestock on the eastern bank, some will run screaming back into the wilderness, some will venture a little way across, see the piled up water and take fright. The hurting ones, the ones in need, those with childlike trust and confidence, will cross over and begin to receive the healing of the abundant kingdom life. Open to the possibility of healing miracles, we start to see them take place.

Kingdom miracles rarely seem to be the result of God reacting to our liturgy, or our skills of persuasion, but they flow abundantly into our response to the love message of Jesus and the news of his provision for us on Calvary. His will to give is never a problem, but our doubts about receiving them may get in the way. Of course, we human beings are unbelievably complicated creatures, and sometimes we do not receive despite all the lessons being learned. As yet there is no final comprehensive answer as to why this is so. Much remains mysterious. But we can now begin. For most of us, the way is now open to start a new journey.

Down the centuries of church history, we have become plagued with alternative ways of thinking —alternative, that is, to the words and works of Jesus. In the context of Scripture, these are all doubts.

In the matter of the distribution of gifts, whatever we Christians say, despite all that has been taught, written and preached, I sometimes say that far too many of us still think of our relationship with God in much the same way as we think of a child's visit to Santa Claus! This illustrates some surprisingly common erroneous thinking: We ask nicely and, if he is all that we think he should be, he will have a present for us. It comes beautifully wrapped, so we may not be able to guess what it is until we get it home. Maybe we unwrap it much later. It could be exactly what we want or something completely unwanted and of no value at all, which we quietly throw away. We cannot go back to him and ask why we did not get the present we wanted, or any gift at all for that matter, as that would seem churlish. At any rate, he rarely seems to speak, so we think we will probably never get a proper explanation as to why we didn't get what we wanted, So we make up an 'answer' for ourselves! Perhaps we might try again another day, perhaps not.

Sadly, that is similar to the sort of pattern many people fall into as they pray. And there are some ministries whose approach elicits that response. We may think that if they ask on our behalf we stand a better chance of obtaining what we need. This 'slot-machine' attitude to God shows up everywhere, and in many different ways. Those of us who speak on public occasions often find that many who need healing queue for ages to be prayed for by the speaker in particular when they often have the most lovely and capable team surrounding them. The presence of Jesus in them is as real as in any of us; the Father loves them just as much when someone else is standing alongside them. But some lessons are hard to learn. We recall that Naaman had a hard lesson to learn. Feeling mightily rejected by Elisha he almost took his leprosy home with him rather than do what the prophet suggested and bathe in the river, all on his own. He nearly lost his healing because of his idolatry directed toward Elisha, or pride in himself. But we must never be judgmental towards supplicants: they have had the opportunity to learn where the speaker stands and what he believes, whereas they will not necessarily know that a good ministry team is made up of Spirit-filled, well-trained people who are also standing in confident faith, trust and agreement. Negative past experiences of ministry can and often do understandably colour people's perceptions.

A major error is to think that we somehow have to discover a road through to God to find his healing. Over such difficult terrain, experts flourish. A 'healing industry' has built up around the erroneous idea that we may have blockages to receiving grace —road blocks and obstacles that have to be circumnavigated or climbed over before we can get there. The effects of our unrepented sins of any kind are often quoted as a cause of failure, strongholds of the enemy holding us back from ever receiving grace. Not to be missed here is the ironic truth that what we deem to be blockages are not blockages at all. Nothing in heaven and earth can come between us and God's love. It is the fact that we have them listed as blockages that creates the blockage. The very existence of such a list makes us doubt that God can work in us, and that doubt gets mightily in the way of things. We are only too ready to proclaim that God's love is unconditional but, when it comes to receiving healing, we do not really believe that at all! Because we have made it all so complicated, we cannot completely surrender to the simple, childlike expectancy of a miracle happening.

Sadly, belief in the 'slot machine' principle runs deeply through parts of the church. So people ask, 'If God wants to heal all who ask, then why didn't so-and-so get healed?' They might as well ask, 'If the slot machine is so loaded to pay out, and the mechanics of the machine are working alright, why did it not do so for her?' Just as corrosive is thinking of God's action as being like a kind of lottery.

It is in times like this when my grasp of the English language is far too inadequate to describe the simple beauty of God's wonderful, restoring kingdom, and our seeming inability to accept it as such. Erroneous thinking is so deeply embedded, inherited and multiplied in its complexity over two thousand years, that my struggling speaking and writing cannot correct it in a moment. We can only make a start.

In the history of the church's healing ministry we can see how recklessly we have squandered our energies and time in brotherly theological 'one-upmanship' between various schools of thought, fruitlessly dissecting things which are often of secondary importance, while the world about us is in such need and the church's great commission only partly fulfilled. I have a deep longing that we would give up hunting for ever more clever philosophical reasons to justify what is seen as failure, and instead devote all that zeal to declaring in the purest simplicity the words and works of Jesus. It is only down that route that the hurt people in the world begin to see healing. We really become servants of God, disciples of Christ, when we do what is commanded of us because it is commanded by him.

It is astonishing to review the vast efforts that have been made over the years to expand what was simplicity itself into what is now enormous complexity, replacing faith with doubt in all areas of belief about a God of restoration, while those ugly, damaging evils of sickness lie outside our gates, and are accepted meekly, like the sick beggar, as part of the landscape!

We must heed the scriptural warnings against lukewarmness, and we must beware of complacency. In the face of discouragements, we must not grow weary. What is needed is a really personal rediscovery of the wonders of the kingdom – the just and gentle rule of God in lives – which is the context for Spirit-filled prayer and Spirit-led ministry.

We generally begin by knowing in our hearts that God is good. But then, if some tragedy threatens our homes and families, there is a tendency to listen to those who readily prophesy over us: 'Not to worry! God is in control!' Control means different things at different levels. At the great level of sustaining all things in being, of course there is one sort of control. In another sense he is indeed in control if our lives are surrendered to him – inasmuch as we really have surrendered to him. (We go on being shown areas where we need to take that further. He has given us a measure of freewill, and only surrender will re-submit that will to his will). But that is not all there is to be said on the matter, as he has given us spiritual weapons of prayer and the word, so we are not just passively to accept disaster or sickness. His will is that we should work with him, according to his will, engaging in spiritual warfare with the biblical weapons he has provided.

So when sickness or injury strike and we are not healed, and we are told by some: 'God has some other purpose; it must be so because he is good and he is in control', whilst it is certainly true that all things work together for good for those who love God, and that God will use us despite unpromising circumstances and afflictions, we really must also remember that sickness is not God's best will for us: he has revealed that he is our healer; it is his nature to bring healing, it is a kingdom dynamic. Moreover, as we saw earlier, we are to focus on his kingdom life rather than supposed blockages to healing.

What about past sin? What about any unforgiveness? Of course Christians need to change from unforgiveness if there is such in their hearts. That is part of the normal Christian life. Of course there are things which offend the Spirit, and we need to get rid of those and cut ourselves off from them: again, such is part of the normal Christian life. But such things cannot be made the basis of kingdom healing, because the focus and the dynamic at work in the healings we see in the pattern of Jesus, and in the apostolic record in Acts, time and time again reveals unmerited grace at work, in that healing is often given regardless of the sufferer's own spiritual position. Others sometimes brought the sick person; sometimes Jesus or apostles were simply moved to heal someone or the sick person just asked and received. Hoops did not have to be jumped through first. In practice, when this truth is not taken on board and reflected in ministry practice, both minister and supplicant really can just go round in circles searching for ever more elusive 'keys', with no satisfactory outcome.

The basic premise that God is good is a great and profound truth, but so much else that men have built ostensibly on that premise is falsehood built on falsehood. God is not the author of sickness; he does not will that people should fall ill or remain ill; sufferers need not be interrogated or 'put on the spot', for none of that is biblically correct. None of it can be found in the spirit of Jesus' ministry to the sick.

Throughout this book, this has been the heart of the matter: the stripping back of all the added man-made theories and steps – built one on top of the other – and returning to the character of Jesus in the Bible who always said yes, with no pre-conditions, to anyone who asked him. Trust in him, and the miraculous appears.

There is another misunderstanding that plagues the church and so badly needs correcting – which is seeing healing ministry as a mechanistic process, like the action of an automatic vending machine. No, when we say that Jesus healed all who asked him or were brought to him, then we must emphasise that the 'asking' is not a ritual to be got right, nor the activation of a machine, but a sincere demonstration of expectancy, a reaction to hearing the good news of Jesus and his kingdom, and a participation in the Spirit-filled life, in which he is at work in and through us.

We must learn to overcome our various doubts and avoid being in any sort of negative position. We may ask for someone to be healed merely because the request is written down on a piece of paper, and because we understand that Jesus responds to request. However it is not only the asking which matters (though of course it does, as we are told by the Lord to ask), but also presence of the mustard seed of positive expectancy. It is when there is expectant faith that we see heaven's gate open over and over again. The Holy Spirit brings gifts, and in step with the Spirit we give glory and honour to Jesus for all that he has done, and is doing, in the continuing life of his kingdom.

So, kingdom walking is very far from a change in ritual, or merely a different way of discussing something we all knew anyway. Neither is it some new way of thinking, or a revamping of well known discussion points. No, kingdom walking entails a positive stripping out of centuries' worth of build up of layer upon layer of bad and unbiblical philosophy —built up to excuse supposed 'failures' in ministry or a supplicant's imagined unworthiness. Doing it a different way, asking a different way —these things will never do it for us. Heaven reveals itself to the opening hearts of the childlike and the spiritually poverty stricken, not to a merely external act of prayer.

So what can I do? Where do I go from here? I have reached a point of understanding in the depths of my soul that healing and forgiveness and love are interrelated; I know that God loves all of us with an equal tenacity, but that we all differ from one another in that we all find love easier or harder to receive. Healing, a manifestation of grace, is similar, in that it pours out of heaven towards all of us and some find it easier than others to receive.

At the moment of Christ's death the curtain in the temple was torn in two, from top to bottom, and the resulting flood of grace into the world was forceful enough to flush into life the dead bodies of the holy ones from their graves. Since that moment God has taken his hand off the tap. The flow of that river is such that he does not make individual decisions about who might be on the receiving end. His love and grace pour freely through that curtain quite irrespective of who might benefit.

God does not make individual decisions about individual supplicants. Just as Calvary was for each and every one of us, so is the healing grace that flows from it.

When we manage to lose our own false images of God, formed out of our own experiences, and strip that image of all the mistaken ideas built up over the centuries, then we begin to see something of the original Jesus, the perfect image of the invisible God. Only then are we able to set aside all the rhetoric about the kingdom and actually see it and walk in it. Then we begin to enter the river of restoring grace that constantly flows from the foot of the cross.

***

The parting of the river Jordan and the Red Sea against their natural tendency, Elijah and Elisha smiting the river with the prophet's cloak to part the waters, Joshua's obedience enacted through the priests —these supernatural acts parted the way for the Israelites. How real are those stories? Can the way be parted for we average human beings who walk in the kingdom today? Is all this real?

The dinghy which carried the pilgrims from the larger boat to the shore ran gently aground about six or eight feet from dry land. The boat was well-laden with people and luggage and the tide was well out. Thoughtful islanders had provided a plank down which our party of pilgrims could step ashore, hopefully undampened by the very slight sea swell between us and the beach. The luggage went ashore, the people went ashore and my guide dog leapt overboard with unbridled enthusiasm which was much more to do with play than pilgrimage! Two strong hands reached on board for me with encouraging shouts of, "Come on, it's your turn!" but they forgot to tell me about the plank. I did not find out until much later that it was there at all. For all I knew at that moment, there was a watery gap between boat and shore and I would simply have to wade through it.

In the general direction of heaven I whispered, "OK, Father, we are just going to have to do this walking on the water stuff, I suppose!"

Out I got, like Peter, with an expectant flourish, onto the surface of the water and stepped straight down through it onto the shingle bottom. The water was about nine or twelve inches deep at this point so it covered my shoes and socks and was well up over my calves. I could feel my trouser bottoms swirling in the slight swell. I only had time to register two quick thoughts: that the water seemed to be exactly at body temperature, and what a horrid job it is to remove cold and soaking wet socks!

I ran and stumbled and splashed ashore, holding tight to the two supporting hands, and reached down to make a first attempt at wringing the wet out of the bottoms of my trousers. I did not have to. They were bone dry. My socks were bone dry and my shoes were bone dry as well. The water had not made me wet!

I thank God this little miracle, this little bit of kingdom fun, this modern day version of Joshua's Jordan adventure, was witnessed by others in our party. I do not claim that I can walk on water because I quite definitely sank. I do not claim that those two outstretched hands must have been ministering angels because I know them and they are, bless them, not that. Nonetheless I was touched very personally by God, who loves to show us just how much he cares and longs to do miracles in our lives.

***

I have always thought of the action of the Spirit of Jesus revealed in the Scriptures as intensely attractive, and his living presence is at work deep inside every kingdom walker. We are drawn by the Spirit, and his pull keeps me heading in the right direction —towards miracles that demonstrate the kingdom when the kingdom is preached. I am hauled out from the shadows of a gnarled and tangled past of cerebral and ineffective healing ministry, into what looks very much like joy.

> To him who sits on the throne and to the Lamb
> be praise and honour and glory and power,
> for ever and ever!
>
> *Revelation 5:13b*